Always a Reason
to Celebrate

Edited by Elizabeth Trotter

Cover design by Ruth Hovsepian

Cover photo by Michele Husfelt; enhanced by Mike Harding

Interior formatting by Lindzee Armstrong

Always a Reason to Celebrate

52 INVITATIONS TO FIND JOY IN GRIEF, LOSS, AND EVERYDAY MOMENTS

MICHELE JO HUSFELT

Contents

To all those who have traveled this journey with me. To my childhood friends, my military family, including my PWOC sisters, and others who have supported and championed my writing journey, I am deeply grateful to every one of you.

To my parents, Patricia Black (1935–2024) and William Black (1934–2024), for an idyllic childhood and an abundance of love at home. I'm so thankful they gave me my sisters, Julee and Laurie, who are the only ones who truly understand what it's like to navigate this new life of celebrating without Mom and Dad. I'm so glad you are my family.

To my five funny kids: Elijah Jay-Michael, Emilie Sara-Grace, Lydia Julee-Anna, Mallory Lindsay-Beth, and Britain Amanda-Rose. From pre-schools in foreign lands to high school and college track and field events, gymnastics meets, dance recitals, living room Bible studies, mission trips, and studies abroad, I have loved every stage of being your mom. Watching you become responsible, neighborly adults who genuinely love and care for those around you has been my greatest joy. May Jesus always be your faithful companion.

To the ones who call me Ammi (rhymes with Mommy): Courtland, Jonah, Charlotte, Hannah, Elizabeth, and Rhett., I never imagined how my heart could nearly burst with delight being your grandmother. Each of you is my very favorite.

And to my beloved, Brother Mike, my greatest cheerleader and earthly treasure, the one who held me close as I cried the first day of classes for my master's in writing and assured me that I would survive.

Throughout all my days, Jesus has been truly faithful, and I have lived in the goodness of God.

Foreword

The year was 2002, the country was Germany, and the occasion was a conference for military wives. It was also God's chosen time and place to bring Michele into my life, for which I am forever grateful.

Married to Mike, a chaplain in the Air Force, Michele was living in Norway but soon moving to Davis-Monthan Air Force Base in Tucson, where I live. Once they arrived, my journey of celebrating life with Michele began. We had two years together, but time and distance have not diminished our friendship. We have managed to be together when possible and have FaceTime tea parties when we can't.

Michele, a mother of five adult children and an animal lover with two Goldendoodles named Hazel Grace and Daisy Jane, possesses a rare ability to share her love for the Lord in a celebratory way that invites others to engage and experience the God who loves them. Her desire to foster community has led her to impact women by initiating fun and practical activities.

While serving as a military spouse, Michele ministered to women all over the world, including a large influx of Afghan refugees fleeing from the Taliban. She established a special lounge for women to meet, provided a hair salon, invited them to tea parties, and celebrated their birthdays.

When she and Mike worked for Apartment Life, a faith-based nonprofit, they held "Yappy Hour" for pets, Easter egg hunts for children and adults, Super Bowl parties, movie nights, neighborhood historical tours, and bagel breakfasts, to name a few. This was a unique way to meet people, connect with the apartment residents, and let neighbors know they were available to help in any way.

Mike is now the pastor of a rural church, and Michele delights in arranging Free Coffee Fridays, ice cream socials, women's teas, evening Bible studies, holiday open houses, and even free popsicle drive-throughs.

Michele is the perfect person to write *Always a Reason to Celebrate.* It's in her DNA to create chances for others to enjoy fellowship, have fun, and experience the love and joy of being a Christian. These short reflections on how God calls us to actively nurture gratitude and joy will motivate, encourage, and give you at least fifty-two reasons to celebrate. Enjoy!

Blessings,
Cynthia Heald
Author of *Becoming a Woman of....* Bible study series

Introduction

In January 2024, I journaled about the new year, sensing it would be a year of "celebration." This word felt fitting as we were planning a 90th birthday party for my dad, which we hoped would be a joyful occasion for him and my mom, who often seemed to project her feelings onto my dad. Mom never wanted Dad to feel excluded (which reflected her own desire not to be left out) and would frequently whisper to us or call us into the kitchen to "make sure we included Dad in our conversations."

A quiet man of few words, he was content to sit in his recliner and listen to the cacophony of his wife and three daughters chatting, laughing, and carrying on. Often, after my mom hung up the phone from an hour-long conversation with one of my sisters or me, my dad would ask, "What did you talk about for an hour?" To which my mom would respond, "Oh, nothing." He did not enjoy being the center of attention, nor did he take great delight in large celebrations. So, more for my mom and the rest of the family, we planned a memorable party for this milestone birthday.

Although I recognized this upcoming time of celebration, I also sensed that the true meaning of this word for the year did not necessarily suggest it would be filled with monumental occasions. Instead, it was a call to find joy and delight in the everyday, sometimes mundane moments of the days ahead. As Richard Foster reminds us in his book, *Celebration of Discipline,* "Scripture commands us to live in a spirit of thanksgiving in the midst of all situations."[1]

March arrived, and we all gathered in Florida to celebrate my dad. His health had been declining for several months, making it a bit more urgent to party while he was still able. The great-grands danced and played, devoured cookies shaped like 90s, sat in Grandad's lap for endless photos with him and my mom, and entertained us by racing my dad's remote cars while he continuously supplied fresh batteries.

The grands participated in The Grandad Trivia Game, featuring twenty-five questions about his childhood in Indiana, his Air Force career, favorite pets, where he and my mom honeymooned, his high school woodworking project (a beautiful boat he built and used for many years), his illustrious college gymnastics awards, how many holes-in-one he made in golf (five!), and who his favorite child was (I'm not sure he had one, but I always claimed it was me). The celebration was exuberant, a glorious day with everyone in attendance enjoying them-selves immensely, especially my dad. He grinned and laughed more enthusiastically than we had seen in a long time. What a day of cele-bration!

And three weeks later, he was gone. The day after the party, he continued his rapid decline. Hospice was called in the following week, and on April 2, he quietly slipped into eternity, holding hands with my mom and eldest sister. We were all in shock yet not surprised. We had spent several months watching him slow down, but no one is ever truly prepared when it happens.

Our new reality involved caring for my mom, who had never lived alone and was grieving the loss of her love of sixty-nine years. (He passed away the day before their anniversary.) She had some health issues, but nothing too serious. A few months later, she had a pacemaker installed to assist with her AFib, and we were desperately searching for the best independent living facility once she was released from rehab.

I had just visited her for the week along with my eldest daughter and

---

1. Richard Foster, *Celebration of Discipline: The Path to Spiritual Growth*, edition. (Place of publication: publisher, year), 194.

youngest grandson. We took two-year-old Rhett to the rehab center, and once inside, he entertained everyone in the corridor leading to her room. He continued to dance, roll, play, talk, jump, and dance some more. Occasionally, he would stop long enough for my mom to hug him and give him a quick kiss or a high five, and then he'd return to his role of entertaining. We celebrated the week and my mom's progress, which would allow her release "in another week or so," according to her doctors and caregivers. They met on Thursday to deliver this good news to my sisters and mom.

On Friday, she didn't feel well when her physical therapist came, so they encouraged her to rest and told her they would return after lunch. She scooted back into bed, turned on the Women's Olympic Gymnastics Finals, and, just before lunch, quietly slipped into the arms of Jesus. We believe she died of a broken heart, four months to the day after losing my dad. Celebrating felt difficult.

In the months following my parents' farewells, I thought about the fact that God intentionally called me to a year of celebration the very same year I lost both my mom and dad. Believing He and His timing are sovereign, I began to ask myself what lessons God wanted to teach me. How does one find joy and celebration in the midst of grief? Why must joy and sorrow walk hand in hand along the path of life? I imagine we won't understand the answers to these and other difficult questions this side of heaven; however, the Lord delights to bestow great joy and peace to us as we find reasons to celebrate even in the midst of deep pain and heartache.

So come journey with me through the everyday and often mundane moments as we seek to celebrate the small yet profound ways God remains present and powerful.

ONE

Celebrate a Word for the Year

Discovering my word for the year was a journey. After a week or so of asking God what it might be and not hearing anything, I reminded myself that the concept of having a word of focus each year is not necessarily biblical and is a relatively new spiritual practice that has gained popularity in recent years. Not wanting to box God in and expect Him to speak or act in a way I thought He should, I continued to trust Him to lead me, whether He gave me a specific theme for the year or not.

That morning, I shared a quote on Facebook that I've been reposting for the last eight years. I was in a bit of a hurry and only skimmed the lines before sitting down to read my devotion for the morning. I'm not sure if God spoke through the words I read or through my time of sitting, listening, and abiding, but the word *celebrate* came to mind. I wrote it in my journal and thought of it throughout the day. I went back to read the quote I had posted, and a few of the lines read, "Expand your horizons. Accumulate experiences. Enjoy the journey. Find every excuse you can to celebrate everything you can."[1] Through various conversations, Scripture, and other readings, I felt God confirm that the year would be one of celebration.

A year of celebration. This doesn't necessarily guarantee great things are going to happen this year. I pray there will be much to celebrate in big ways, but more specifically, I believe the focus will be on celebrating the small things; searching in the everyday and mundane to find glimpses of the Holy; finding cause for celebration when circumstances would not normally warrant bringing out the sparkling cider and balloons; celebrating small wins that may eventually lead to big wins, but if not, remembering the celebration of the small was still worth it.

I recently finished a book called *The Power to Change* by Craig Groeschel. In it, he encourages us to note our "wins" throughout the process of forming and implementing new habits. We don't have to wait until we achieve a significant milestone to celebrate a win. Each time we choose a right response, we can check that off in the "win" column. Up until now, I have not written a book. Yet every time I choose to sit down and write, I win! Most of our goals require moving through a process. And almost every process is filled with many opportunities to celebrate small wins along the way. There are few examples where there is no cause for celebration until the very end. (Except, perhaps, the book of Job!)

Yesterday, we talked to our daughter in Africa. I celebrated technology, her safety in a vulnerable location, and new friends for my grandchildren to play with. After church, we went to lunch with a new couple. In my heart, I celebrated new relationships and the financial means to treat our friends to lunch.

Today I wrote an essay. Win! My house is not clutter-free, but my living room is. Yay! I haven't put away all the dishes, but I washed the crockpot and put it back on the shelf. Good job! And I haven't read the Bible through, but today I completed day nine of my year-long plan. Yes! What a day to celebrate!

What do you need to celebrate today? What circumstances have clouded your vision and caused you to miss seeing glimpses of the Holy

---

1. Mark Batterson, *All In: You Are One Decision Away from a Totally Different Life.* (Zondervan, 2015), 98.

in your everyday existence? I pray that as you read about the ways I have seen God and the numerous reasons to celebrate, you, too, will refocus your sights and ask God to reveal His acts of kindness and compassion, His grace and mercy that are often easy to miss along our often busy and chaotic journey.

So let's bring out the bubbly (or grape juice or cider) and the balloons and begin to discover anew and exclaim just like the Israelites upon their return from Babylonian captivity, "We were filled with laughter, and we sang for joy. And the other nations said, 'What amazing things the Lord has done for them.' 'Yes, the Lord has done amazing things for us! What joy!'" (Ps. 126:2–3).

TWO

Celebrate a New Year

I wrote the Christmas card and tucked the gift card inside. Then I wrote her name on the envelope and attached a string through a tiny hole. "Dear Friend, this is a gift with a string attached. Should you choose to play along, this gift card can only be used when we visit this coffeehouse together. In other words, time spent together is really the gift. (So, perhaps this is really a gift to me, as well!) Merry Christmas! Love, Michele."

Thinking I was clever, I told my daughter about this gift idea. She smiled a cute but sarcastic smile and said, "Mom, do you really think spending time with you is a gift? Like, do you really think you're a gift?" She made me laugh.

When thinking about the new year and a fresh start, I sat down to pray and ponder about what I'd like the new year to look like. What changes do I want to make? What are some ways I can make a difference?

I decided I wanted this year's changes to focus not on self-improvement or what I can do to better myself, but rather, changes that will make a difference in others' lives. This year I want to be intentional to care more for those around me, to invest in the community(s) God has gifted me with. I want my life to make others' lives better.

To that end, these five attributes encompass what I want the new year to include:

1. To be more generous. You've heard the old (but true) saying, "You can't outgive God." This year I want to test Him on this. I pray my giving would be marked by sacrifice and great joy. I pray for new and creative ways to give generously—not only financially, but by the generous giving of praise, encouragement, kindness, and time.

2. To be more kind—to have or show a friendly, generous, and considerate nature. I want to be like Tabitha, who lived in Joppa and was mentioned in Acts 9:36: "She was always doing kind things for others and helping the poor." I don't want to win the approval of others, but to simply live out of the abundance of kindness the Lord and others have shown me.

3. To be more encouraging. "You can do this!" "I am for you!" "God is bigger than this insurmountable mountain you're facing!" "I understand." "I'm so sorry." "I've been there, too." "Let's pray." One of the most encouraging stories in Scripture is that of Aaron and Hur as they encourage Moses. While Joshua led the troops into battle, Moses, along with Aaron and Hur, watched the battle from a nearby hill. Exodus 17:11 reads, "As long as Moses held up the staff in his hand, the Israelites had the advantage. But whenever he dropped his hand, the Amalekites gained the advantage." As Moses became weary both physically and mentally, Aaron and Hur took their places on either side of Moses and held his arms high. We all need people in our lives who walk beside us and lift us up. This year I want to be more of an encourager to those around me.

4. To be less critical. I told a friend about this conviction to be less critical and came to understand how personal a goal this really is. A critical spirit may manifest itself differently in each person. It all comes down to spending time with Jesus, asking Him to reveal our heart and motives. For me, a

critical spirit is usually birthed out of thinking that someone else isn't doing a task the way I would have done it. That my way is the better way. This year I want to value others' opinions and ideas and walk with an open heart and open hands. I want to hold my ministries, projects, ideas loosely, ready to give up ownership when needed, especially to honor others.

5. To give the gift of time. Lastly, I want to give those around me my most valuable asset, my time. Granted, not everyone's love language is the gift of quality time, but I believe we all could benefit from a little time spent with a friend. When I decorated our farmhouse in Ohio, one of the first things I did was add a sign above the doorway in the kitchen that read, "Never too busy for friendship or tea." I cringe when people tell me I'm too busy. I may have a full schedule and lots of things on my calendar, but I never want anyone to think I'm too busy to spend time with them. People are one of the few eternal treasures we get to invest in. They are where I want to spend my time.

This year, I want to see others more clearly and dedicate my time and resources to make those around me feel encouraged, loved, and recognized. I trust the Lord to nurture these five qualities in my life as I seek ways to grow.

Celebrate While We Wait

I'm sitting by a window peering into the backyard, watching raindrops dance on the patio table. I'm waiting.

The tiny onesies have been washed and folded neatly and are waiting. The quiet bedroom filled with tiny human belongings, his name hanging above the crib and the chair that longs to rock him to sleep. They're waiting.

My daughter balances her empty coffee cup on her round belly while she reads her Bible.

She's waiting.

A large picture window expands the length of the living room, and we watch the world carry on outside while we continue to wait.

Trusting in God's timing. It sounds spiritual and wise. The truth is, it's hard. Scripture reminds us again and again to "Trust in the Lord with all your heart; do not depend on your own understanding" (Prov. 3:5). Isaiah 26:3 assures us, "You will keep in perfect peace all who trust in you, all whose thoughts are fixed on you!" And Psalm 37:5 reminds us, "Commit everything you do to the Lord. Trust him, and he will help you." The truth is, it's really hard to wait. I'm learning it's like almost anything that is worthwhile to achieve; it takes practice.

I know I'm not alone in the waiting. I have friends who are waiting for their next military assignment. It's never easy to wait patiently to hear where you'll spend the next several years or if the military will continue to be part of your journey at all.

Some are waiting to hear where their child will go to university or *if* their child will go to university.

Some are waiting for a lost child to come home.

One friend is waiting for a life-threatening surgery as a last resort for her husband. I was one who, until recently, was waiting for my husband to return from a long deployment in a war-torn location.

What might you be waiting for?

Perhaps an equally important question I'm learning to ask myself is, "What might you be learning in the waiting?"

My prayer is evolving from asking God when He will answer to asking what He's trying to teach me while I wait.

I don't want to waste the moments of today simply waiting. I want God to use the moments and days to teach me. I'm learning just how faithful He is in the waiting. He reminds me of His love as I have time to sit and read and ponder His Word. He reminds me of others I can pray for and come alongside as they wait.

I see community rise to embrace me in the waiting. A card or message from a friend that says I'm thinking of you and lifting you to the Father. A group of friends invite us for lunch, to sit around the table and commune together and enjoy the laughter of the little ones who jump on the couch and talk a mile a minute, who are eager to eat one more bite of chicken so they can have another helping of macaroni.

I'm learning to be grateful for the expectant father who caters to my sweet daughter. Who brings her flowers on her due date. Who gently holds her and sits and watches girly shows when he'd rather be out in the garage. Who dreams out loud of renovating his workshop so he and his son can work on projects together, building dirt bikes and memories, just like he did with his dad.

I'm learning to enjoy and savor the extra time with my daughter. Having five children doesn't always afford a mom a lot of time with each child. God is reminding me how special this time is with my dancing darling middle child, my own flesh who is waiting to birth our next generation.

As my daughter and I walk each day, God reminds me of His beauty in creation and His love to share it with me. The tall evergreen trees towering over the landscape here in the Pacific Northwest. The calmness of Puget Sound holding its water within the boundaries of the banks. The snow-capped mountains standing so proudly in the background. So many reminders of gentle graces to capture in the waiting. I don't want to miss the tiniest of them.

I pray today will be the day baby Jonah makes his grand entrance. But if not, I'll continue to be thankful for what God is teaching me. I'll savor the moments and walk through each day wide-eyed, full of hope and grateful for what I am learning. And I'll continue to trust Him in His timing, always remembering His goodness and faithfulness.

FOUR

Celebrate Someday

For most of you, today was Saturday. But for me, it was Someday.

I left work in D.C., and what should have taken me three and a half hours to get home took me seven hours. Because it was Someday.

I've taken the back roads home before, and as I passed little antique shops in tiny towns, I would say to myself, "Someday, I'm going to stop in those little shops." I passed a beautiful Methodist church and whispered, "Someday, I want to stop and take pictures of its door. And the cross that faces the field."

As I drove north on Hwy 213, I came to the crossroads of Main Street in Cecilton and told myself, "Someday, I'm going to take a detour and drive by my husband's grandparents' home and reminisce about all the ice cream we ate on their front porch."

"Someday, instead of passing over the Chesapeake City Bridge, I'm going to go under it to see what's on the other side," I declared to myself.

So, guess what? Today was my Someday. I stopped in those little shops and met friendly locals and told them that my husband was born just up the road.

It was drizzling and dreary when I came to the Methodist church, but I pulled over, got out of my car and took those pictures. I took a left onto Main Street in Cecilton and stopped to take a picture of Mike's grandparents' house. I pulled into his elementary school to turn around. When I reached the drawbridge a little further ahead, I had to stop so a boat could pass through the water!

And I was tickled to drive under the bridge in Chesapeake City and get a glimpse of a beautiful wedding party, including the new bride and groom.

I'm so grateful today was Someday. And I look forward to adding more of them to my calendar in the days ahead.

FIVE

Celebrate Tripp's Dad

Dear Tripp's Dad,

On behalf of mothers everywhere, I want to thank you for helping my daughter today. As she stood behind her car, trying to figure out how to maneuver an awkwardly large box from her trunk into the store, you came along, hand in hand with your son, Tripp.

First, you noticed my daughter and her dilemma. More importantly, you went out of your way to help her. You cheerfully announced that you would trade her positions: if she held Tripp's hand, you would carry her box.

She gladly accepted, and Tripp willingly transferred his hand from yours to hers. (You've obviously taught Tripp to trust your judgment and that not all strangers are dangerous.)

They walked and talked together across the parking lot and into Crate & Barrel. You came in behind them, and as you set the box on the counter, the cashier asked how she could help you all. And you replied, "Well, it looks like my part is done now." You smiled at Tripp, clasped his hand in yours, and off the two of you went. I'm sure you didn't think of all the people you impacted by your small gesture of helping my daughter.

Obviously, you had great impact on my daughter, who, in turn, called me with the good news that there are still nice people in the world who are willing to take a few minutes to put others first. I'd be willing to bet there were others in the parking lot who watched as you came to the rescue. They would have surmised you didn't know my daughter and how easily you could have walked down another aisle and been on your way. After all, everyone is so busy. Everyone would have understood.

And the cashier. I'm sure she was confused when you came in, plopped the big box on the counter and announced that your job was done. She likely told a co-worker or friend about what this man did at work today.

And here I am sharing your story with friends and other people I've never met, simply because they've come across these pages. Many of them are literally scattered across the world. You probably thought you were only impacting one young lady living in Atlanta.

Not the least of those impacted by your kindness, though, is your son, Tripp. As he grows up, he will undoubtedly be aware of those around him who need a little extra help. He will know what it means to be a real gentleman in a world where real gentlemen are rare. After all, that's the example his father taught him.

So, again, thank you, Tripp's Dad. You've brought a lot of smiles and warmed a lot of hearts with your willingness to take a few minutes out of your busy life to simply lend a helping hand.

SIX

Celebrate a Need

The kids were clapping their hands and grinning from ear to ear as they made their way into the big church building. I found myself caught up in their excitement and fumbled for my phone, wanting to capture the scene before me.

We were visiting my daughter and son-in-law one Sunday morning, and as we made our way from the side of the building, we noticed several little red wagons parading through the parking lot. As we got closer, I realized they were being pulled by volunteers making their way to the parked minivans, SUVs, and four-door sedans. Parents were unbuckling car seats, handing over diaper bags and dinosaur backpacks, and unloading little ones who were anticipating their magical ride in a little red wagon, right up to the front doors of the church. Ingenious, I thought.

Someone saw a need.

My sweet friend has breast cancer. As I was perusing the shop trying to find a warm blanket or shawl to send her, I remembered a ministry at my sister's church. Several of her friends gather each week and spend the morning knitting beautiful shawls to gift to those in need of a warm, enveloping reminder that someone cares—and mostly that Jesus cares. The ladies pray over the shawls and attach a little note to each one, so the recipient knows the love and care and prayers that have gone into the heartwarming creations. The shawls are taken to nursing homes, chemo centers, hospitals, and any other place someone needs a warm touch. So tenderly beautiful, I thought.

Someone saw a need.

Who has a need in your little circle? What ways could you creatively share a touch from Jesus today?

I visited an elderly friend today. She shared with me how lonely her Sunday evenings are. Her husband has passed away, and she particularly misses him on Sundays. She comes home from church and eats lunch, and then her day seems to go downhill because of her loneliness. As we talked, the Lord opened my eyes to see a need.

Hebrews 6:10 reminds us, "God is not unjust; he will not forget your work and the love you have shown him as you have helped his people and continue to help them."

"Dear Jesus, thank you for all those around us who have the ability to see the needs and take action. Would you grant me the insight to recognize the needs of those around me? In small ways, or perhaps in grander ones, help me to be a blessing to someone today. Amen."

SEVEN

Celebrate a First Response

I admire first responders, most likely because I know I could never be one. I can't imagine the responsibility of being the first on the scene of an accident and having to assess the situation and respond accurately. Never mind the fact that I faint at the sight of blood. It would not be good.

While I could never be a first responder, lately I'm becoming more aware of my need to have the proper first response. In many situations recently, I've noticed that my first response is not what it should be, and I end up having to go back to reevaluate and respond correctly the second time.

Case in point: I had plans to spend the day bike riding. When I went down to unlock my bike, my key would not work. Rather than a godly first response that would acknowledge God as the director of my day and trust that He had better plans for me, I felt frustration taking over my thoughts and actions.

Later when someone asked me to complete a task I didn't want to do, my first response was to think, "I don't have time for that. And it's not as important as what I had planned." As soon as I thought this, I had to reevaluate and formulate a better second response: "Sure. It's not what I had planned, but that's okay. I am happy to help with whatever you need."

I'm discovering that my first response is usually a selfish one. Given time and another chance, I'm fairly good at responding correctly the second time around. But I hear the Lord reminding me that my first response should be the one that is pleasing to Him.

So my prayer these days is that I would get it right the first time. That, indeed, I would be an excellent first responder after all.

EIGHT

Celebrate a Beautiful Inheritance

I was so excited to discover that my condition is real and even has a name. Hello, my name is Michele, and I'm an Anglophile. According to Wikipedia, an Anglophile is a person who admires England, its people, and its culture.

While living in England, I remember the narrow, winding roads, the gardens, fresh milk delivered to our doorstep, the High Street, and fabulous tea. I fell in love with the monarchy, especially the pageantry and pomp and circumstance. We attended the Queen's Jubilee, visited Buckingham Palace and Sandringham (the UK's version of Camp David), and were always on the lookout for a glimpse of royalty.

As I was reading my Bible the other day, I came across this in Galatians 3:29: "And now that you belong to Christ, you are the true children of Abraham. You are his heirs, and God's promise to Abraham belongs to you." And another one in Galatians 4:7: "Now you are no longer a slave but God's own child. And since you are his child, God has made you his heir."

For some reason, I started thinking of Queen Elizabeth and Princess Mia of Genovia (from *The Princess Diaries*), wondering, "Do they wake up every morning having forgotten they are royalty? Do they need to be reminded they are heirs to the throne, that they have special rights and privileges simply because they belong to the royal family? Not because of who they are, or what they've done, but only because of whose they are?"

There are many verses that remind me I'm an heir. According to Ephesians 3:6, "This mystery is that through the gospel, the Gentiles are heirs together with Israel, members together of one body, and sharers together in the promise in Christ Jesus" (NIV). And again in Titus 3:7, we read, "So that, having been justified by his grace, we might become heirs having the hope of eternal life" (NIV).

So why do I have to be reminded that I'm an heir and that I have a beautiful inheritance? Why do I wake up so often in the morning and trudge through my day without the slightest thought of who I really am and the benefits that come from who I really am? I want to live with a constant awareness that I have access to the throne of Almighty God, not because of anything I've done but simply because I belong to Him. The rights and privileges that I am afforded should be enough to keep me content, to keep me joyful and expectant, to remind me that in Christ, I am secure and safe. I can walk in freedom and assurance because, indeed, "The land you have given me is a pleasant land. What a wonderful inheritance!" (Ps. 16:6).

NINE

Celebrate Lessons Learned

I just listened to a friend share her story at her church, and I'm now sitting with many jumbled thoughts and feelings. She was inspiring. Through many difficult challenges and circumstances, she kept her eyes on Jesus as He remained faithful.

She was honest and vulnerable. At many heartbreaking bends and devastating diagnoses, she asked questions most of us have whispered but are not brave enough to voice to others. "Oh, God, why?" And "How much longer?" And "Not again! How much more can I take?"

Yet she never gave up, though she suffered two miscarriages, two different cancers, another health issue resulting in being wheelchair-bound for a year, the deaths of her parents and brother, a bout with depression, and the loss of a precious baby girl at the age of four days. (The Lord did give her the miracle of two other beautiful daughters who have smiles one would need a yardstick to measure. What a gift as she was told she would never be able to have children due to one of the cancer treatments.) Through it all, even when enveloped with doubt and fear, her Savior remained faithful.

As I listened to her share, I beamed with pride. After all, she was one of "my" PWOC gals. (Protestant Women of the Chapel is a ministry to women on military installations worldwide. I affectionately refer to the many younger women with whom I've walked during different assignments as "my" girls.) We journeyed together for two years, gathering weekly (minus several months during COVID) and seeing each other around the base. Yet after hearing her testimony, I sadly realized I didn't really know her. I had no idea the abyss she had lived through.

As I listened to her testimony, I was reminded of our time together in New Jersey. Quiet and attentive, she knew and loved Jesus. She was extremely reliable and cheerfully willing to lend a hand wherever she was needed, whether it be in the kitchen or the children's rooms. The girl I remembered was kind and gentle with a heart to serve, yet I didn't understand the depth of her loss and the brokenness out of which she had risen.

As I finished listening to her story, I was encouraged and inspired by the strength of her faith. But I was also sad. Sad that I had not taken the time to learn this sweet sister's story. Sad that I had not been aware of the many anniversaries of loss she silently suffered in those years we were together. Grateful she had a supportive family and other friends who knew her, yet sad I was not aware and able to offer comfort when she may have needed an extra dose.

I sit and ponder the many lessons the Lord has revealed to me as I reflect on hearing my friend's story. I ask God for His eyes to see those around me more clearly. Scripture is clear that we need each other. Ecclesiastes 4:9–10 reminds us that "Two people are better off than one, for they can help each other succeed. If one person falls, the other can reach out and help. But someone who falls alone is in real trouble." Most of all, I pray I will be more intentional to create space and moments where others feel safe and loved and free to share their stories.

Thank you, Friend, for bravely sharing yours with me and so many others. May we all come to understand the power of each other's stories.

TEN

Celebrate the Finish Line

Even if it's a terrible book, I still feel the need to finish reading once I've started. I covet completed projects and hesitate to start a new task before the current one is checked off my list. I confess, in most cases I'm not an advocate for multi-tasking. I'm not very good at it, and my judgmental heart exerts little grace to those who pretend they're engaged in conversation with me yet are distracted by their phones, pings, and other interferences. In my tiny world, finishing something is simply common sense. (If it sounds like I'm in a boxing match with pride, I'll admit, I am.)

After engaging in an interesting conversation with my boss, Katie, I found myself reflecting on the idea of finishing. She shared from a book where the author challenged readers to finish what they start. As she recited examples such as hanging up your robe after you're dressed, putting things away after a task, wiping the table after lunch, and filing papers that are no longer needed, I mentioned to her how these are all simply common sense.

The Lord has shown me how I often need to be reminded of common-sense ideas. As I moved through the next week, I noticed tasks I hadn't finished. I noticed that we finished dinner, but dinner wasn't really finished until the dishes were cleaned and put away. I thought I was finished with my walk, but my shoes needed to be returned to the closet before my walk was complete.

In little tasks and in the important ones, I want to finish things. And finish things well. As Ecclesiastes 7:8 reminds us, "Better is the end of a thing than its beginning, and the patient in spirit is better than the proud in spirit" (ESV).

ELEVEN

Celebrate the Radical

My pregnant daughter, son-in-law, and three grandchildren lived in a camper as they helped another couple care for their eighteen adopted children. Both families are living radical lives. My daughter and her family have since moved overseas to a climate with temperatures over 100 degrees and no air conditioning. That sounds radical, as well.

Another friend gave up a very successful military career and moved his family to a small village in India. He is one of a few surgeons tirelessly treating the downtrodden and extremely impoverished. Existing from day to day, unsure of their next paycheck amid government unrest, their calling includes much sacrifice and suffering. They are living radically.

We all know people who have chosen to take the uncharted course, to live what I would term *radically*. According to the world's standards, their lifestyles make little sense. Why would they intentionally endure hardship? How do they expect to get ahead? Build a nest egg? Provide for their children to attend college? In a comfort-driven "me" culture, these unconventional lifestyles often invoke three contrasting responses: intrigue, envy, and guilt.

I find myself intrigued at what drew them to color outside the lines.

Was it a certain personality or character trait that caused them to be dissatisfied with the status quo? Or was it a uniquely discerning Spirit that enabled them to sense God calling them out from the ordinary? Always interested in someone's story and the motivation behind their actions, I find myself intrigued by those who determine to live radically according to the world's standards.

Along with intrigue, I confess I'm often envious of those who are willing to buck tradition and expectations to radically follow Jesus, who choose a non-traditional approach to their sense of purpose and calling. There is a steadfastness in their step and a confident determination to blaze a new trail without caring if anyone else follows. Not concerned with leading or following, they set off on a journey with the companions of uncertainty, risk, loneliness, misunderstanding, financial and physical hardship, and overall great sacrifice. These characteristics remind me of Paul and certainly of Jesus. Oh, to have the faith of Isaiah as he exclaimed, "Here I am. Send me" (Is. 6:8). Or to follow obediently like Abraham, who left his home and country and set out for a land God would show him. These and many more depict radical lifestyles and noble examples to follow.

As I read Scripture or books or hear stories of those living counter-culturally, I sometimes also find myself wrestling with feelings of guilt. Should I sell everything I have and give it all to the poor? Must I move to Africa and live in a jungle to show how much I love Jesus? Perhaps God would be most pleased if I spent my days walking the streets laden with a heavy wooden cross atop my back, sweat pouring down my brow, while passing out tracts to those who stop to inquire about my radical lifestyle.

I'm reminded of the story in Acts when the believers sold everything they had and had everything in common. Does that make you just a little nervous as it does me, that Jesus might call me to do something so radical?

The reality, though, is that Jesus *is* calling each of us to live radically. Forgiving those who hurt us or harm our children is one way He calls us to live radically. When Jesus taught his disciples to turn the other cheek, they were given a challenge to respond counter-culturally by not retaliating or attempting to get even. I realized this in a recent conversation about another religion's teaching of "an eye for an eye." When someone insults their god, severe punishment, including death, is required. The concept of forgiveness is foreign to those who follow this religion. In contrast, following Jesus' demonstration of forgiveness to those who hurt us is a radical response.

Whether we have plenty or live in need, enjoy comfort or endure challenging circumstances, we are all called to live counter-culturally. How might God be calling you to a radical way of life?

TWELVE
Celebrate This Unlikely Adventure

The packers have driven away with all our worldly possessions, and I sit in an almost empty house on a couch that, if possession really is nine-tenths of the law, belongs to our Goldendoodle, Hazel Grace. With no room in our new residence, this treasure will need to find a new home within the next day or two as we clean around it, preparing for our final inspection of a military house. The final inspection of a military house—a daunting thought. As all good things must come to an end, we are turning the pages on the last chapter of our military career. But today we focus on the new adventure.

Many friends have journeyed with us over the past three years as we have sought the Lord's direction for what comes next. Feeling excited and confident, two years ago we made an offer on a home in Lancaster County, envisioning it as a hospitality house or bed and breakfast. It features two acres with a meandering creek and beautiful views of a neighboring Amish farm. The offer was accepted, and negotiations volleyed back and forth until we had an agreed-upon closing date. However, as the day approached, the owners backed out. A door closed.

Disappointed yet trusting God, we continued our search throughout Lancaster County. We placed a bid on an Amish farm, and even though we didn't win, we became friends with the owners! We spent countless weekends visiting homes and often dropped what we were doing on weekday afternoons to drive two hours for a potential opportunity. While I can't provide an exact number, we looked at nearly fifty homes or current bed and breakfasts. Ultimately, all the doors closed.

Meanwhile, the two directors at the organization I work for in Virginia mentioned several times a small country church whose pastor was retiring. Ironically, I had visited this church a few years ago during an off-site workday. Since then, my immediate boss, Katie, would occasionally say how crazy it would be if God called us to that church or one of our other country churches in the association. The thought was amusing; however, retirement taxes are high in Virginia, and we could never afford to live in that specific area. Besides, God was calling us to Lancaster.

We continued to pursue our dream of Lancaster while the thought of Virginia lingered in our minds behind the Amish buggies. Mike accepted a call to preach at a small church in March, purely out of obedience, knowing we could back out as soon as we found a home in Lancaster. To be honest, although it was a lovely church in a beautiful area surrounded by horse farms and wineries, the idea of pastoring a church was never among our preferred options after military retirement. We felt called to some form of ministry, but pastoring a church was not on the list.

Still lacking a solid lead in Lancaster, Mike preached that Sunday in March. We met the seven-member remnant of a once-thriving congregation, several of whom represented six generations of members. They were warm and welcoming. Determined not to let their church and community presence die, they have fought with grit to move forward. We left that morning in the drizzling rain, unsure how, but fully aware that God was changing our hearts toward this church and community. As they reminisced about past ecumenical events with the three other churches in town, we began to share their vision for reaching the community rather than solely filling the pews on Sunday mornings.

The concept of establishing a Kingdom community with Methodists, Episcopalians, and African American Baptists generated new excitement about what God might be doing. With each subsequent visit, our confirmation continued to grow, and despite our determination to find a place in Lancaster, each door clearly closed.

As we prepare to relocate to the quaint "Village of Upperville," with a population of 129, located just outside of Paris (Virginia!), we leave New Jersey with a renewed belief that God is doing a new thing—somewhat typical of how He often works, which may not make sense. We continue to hold on to the hope for Lancaster one day, but for now, we are eager to experience the goodness of the Lord nestled in the Piedmont horse country. Please come visit us soon; we'll be running an unofficial bed and breakfast. You'll find us at "The Baptist Pastorium" on Highway 50 in Upperville, just two doors down from the British Pub and right outside of Paris.

THIRTEEN

Celebrate the Silence

Reading in the book of Job one morning, I stopped to ponder Job 2:13. Satan began to sift Job, and in the midst of his discouragement, three of his friends came to visit. The verse reads, "Then they sat on the ground with him seven days and nights, but no one spoke a word to him because they saw that his suffering was very intense" (CSB).

When we lived in Southern California, a friend and I would drive the three hours to L.A. to sightsee, attend an occasional conference, or visit another friend. We were quite content to be together without needing to constantly talk. We might turn on the music and occasionally make a comment, but we found comfort and camaraderie in simply being together, free from unnecessary chatter. On one occasion, we invited another friend to join us, someone who felt the need to quickly fill any silent moment with a litany of pointless remarks. We found ourselves secretly yet jointly battling the urge to say to her, "Can you just be quiet and enjoy our company?"

Job's friends came to provide comfort during his suffering. The most effective time of encouragement and compassion during their visit was the first seven days, when they simply sat with him in silence. Ironically, on the eighth day when they began to talk, their poor advice and lack of wisdom began a downhill spiral that certainly did not benefit or uplift Job's spirits.

I recently met a woman on a flight to D.C. who was on her way to visit a friend who is terminally ill. One of her concerns was the conversation she would have with her friend. She was anxious about what she might say to bring comfort and encouragement. I suggested that while words can often be appropriate and what we say matters, many times comfort comes from silence and simply being present. There is freedom in knowing you don't always need to have the right words. Let's celebrate the gift of being together and sharing the silence, especially in times when God is deeply at work.

FOURTEEN

Celebrate the Sabbath

I've always admired the women at the tomb who stopped to observe the Sabbath before preparing Jesus' body for burial. Jesus died Friday afternoon before sundown. As was the Jewish law, Shabbat, or Sabbath, began at sundown Friday and concluded at sundown Saturday. During this twenty-four-hour period, the Jews adhered to very strict rules including no cooking, cleaning, or any type of work. There was even a limit to the number of steps they could walk. Mark 16:1 tells us, "When the Sabbath was over, Mary Magdalene, Mary the mother of James, and Salome bought spices so that they might go to anoint Jesus' body" (NIV).

I imagine how difficult it would have been for the women to leave Jesus' body while they went home and rested in observance of the Sabbath. What could be more important than caring for Jesus immediately after His brutal death? Even though the Sabbath was an ingrained custom, I'm sure the women considered this an urgent situation that could perhaps warrant an exception to the rule this one time.

What has intrigued me even further has been the recent "aha" moment of realizing that not only did the women stop to rest, but Jesus Himself observed that same Sabbath. Jesus died on Friday. His body rested on Saturday. And He rose again on Sunday. Scripture doesn't tell us Jesus waited until the third day to be raised from the dead to observe the Sabbath; however, we know the Sabbath was an important rhythm God desired for His people. I wonder if this was part of God's plan to remind us of our need to rest. When the world desperately needed good news, Jesus remained in the tomb, confident of God's timing.

Mark 2:27 reminds us, "The Sabbath was made for man, not man for the Sabbath" (NIV). Sabbath isn't a list of dos and don'ts; it is an invitation from God to stop striving, to take a break, to create a rhythm of resting and relaxing in Him, and to focus on delighting in our relationship with our Heavenly Father. There will always be important tasks that seem urgent, but God bids us to stop. Not when our to-do list is complete, but perhaps in the middle of our list so we can experience His provision and presence.

When time seems of the essence, He longs to remind us to cease striving and to be still. Throughout Scripture, we see examples of God and His people including a rhythm of rest in their daily routine. As we reflect on Christ's sacrifice for us, may we ponder our observance of the Sabbath to discover more fully how He calls us to delight and rest in Him.

FIFTEEN

Celebrate My Favorite Child

On each of my children's birthdays, I address cards "To My Favorite Child." When they were younger, it was easy to call "The Boy" (our affectionate name for Eli) our favorite son, as he was the only one. However, trailing him were four daughters, all eager to be the favorite as well.

I would hear other parents who carefully told their children they didn't have a favorite, that they loved all their children equally. How disappointing, I thought. Doesn't every child long to be their parents' favorite?

As they grew up, I decided early on that the one I was with would be my favorite. As Britain and I drove home from school, I would comment to her, "Britain, you're my favorite child." She would beam in response. When Mallory came in from practice, I'd greet her at the door, give her a hug, and remind her that she was my favorite child. At a track meet, when Eli sat his sweaty body next to me in the bleachers, I would hand him a towel and exclaim, "Eli, you are my favorite child." Lydia would dance through the kitchen and down the hall, and I would sing as she pirouetted, "There goes Lydia, my favorite child." When Emilie called me from college for the fourth time that day, I would answer the phone and cheerfully say, "Hello, Emilie, my favorite child."

My children are all grown now and beginning to have children of their own. I cherish the adult conversations we share and enjoy listening to the memories they recount from their childhood. Interestingly, not long ago, Mallory and Lydia engaged in a playful debate about who they each believed was my favorite child. I simply smiled.

God our Father has many children. And He longs for us to know that we are His very favorite. He doesn't love us equally; He loves us individually, as if we were His one and only child.

On days when I feel unlovable, I need only open my Bible, His personal love letter to me, and read a few of His thoughts. With a love that is vastly immeasurable, the Father exclaims to each one of us, "You are my favorite child!"

See what great love the Father has lavished on us, that we should be called children of God!
And that is what we are!

— *1 JOHN 3:1 NIV*

SIXTEEN

Celebrate When It's More Than You Can Handle

W e often hear the well-meaning but unbiblical phrase, "God won't give you more than you can handle," as an adage or encouragement to those struggling through a tough time. It is simply untrue. The oft-misquoted verse here is 1 Corinthians 10:13, which states that God will not allow us to be tempted beyond what we can handle.

When writing to the Corinthians, Paul expressed the dire state he and his companions were in during their travels through Asia: "We were under great pressure, far beyond our ability to endure, so that we despaired of life itself. Indeed, we felt we had received the sentence of death. But this happened that we might not rely on ourselves but on God, who raises the dead" (2 Cor. 1:8-9 NIV). Paul was convinced that without the strength and power of God, they would not have made it; their circumstances were more than they could handle.

Recently, while reading the account of the crucifixion, I was struck by who was proclaiming He could not handle the situation on His own. Jesus, in His humanity, bore the sins of the world. In the garden, He prayed that God would take away the intense suffering and the impending sentence of death. But He submitted to the will of the

Father, relying solely on God's strength. The next few days would be more than He could bear.

We live in a broken world filled with grief and suffering. There will be challenges and circumstances, whether due to our own actions or not, that we will not be able to handle successfully without calling on the name of the Lord. Paul continued, "He has delivered us from such a deadly peril, and he will deliver us again. On him we have set our hope that he will continue to deliver us" (2 Cor. 1:10 NIV). We cannot rely on our own strength. Left to our own devices, God often gives us more than we can handle.

My prayer for each of us is that we will remember and rejoice in the assurance that Paul reminds us of in Ephesians: "I pray that the eyes of your heart may be enlightened in order that you may know the hope to which he has called you, the riches of his glorious inheritance in his holy people, and his incomparably great power for us who believe. That power is the same as the mighty strength he exerted when he raised Christ from the dead and seated him at his right hand in the heavenly realms" (Eph. 1:18–20 NIV). These are especially great thoughts on the days God gives us more than we can handle.

SEVENTEEN

Celebrate Resurrection Hope

I recently attended a retreat, and as I observed the women sitting in the large circle, I became curious about the journey each of them took to arrive in that particular seat, in this particular location, "for such a time as this."

Later that day, I conducted a survey that lacked scientific rigor and simply asked several women how they ended up at our retreat. Not surprisingly, most said they were invited by someone else. They received personal invitations. One lady saw an advertisement on Facebook, while another found it in the church bulletin. The majority, however, were invited by a friend, fellow churchgoer, or Bible study attendee. Invitations are important.

The beginning of Holy Week stirs up many personal thoughts. I spend a few extra minutes each morning contemplating what this week looked like to Jesus. Pondering His suffering and agony and anticipation of becoming broken for us, I am also reminded of my friends and neighbors who haven't yet experienced His great love for our very broken world.

How do they go on? How do those without a personal relationship with and faith in Jesus continue to walk in this fallen world with all the aches, pains, and hopelessness that naturally accompany a journey through this life? I wrestle with these questions often as I look out my window and walk down my street. I imagine the hurt, disappointment, and suffering that takes place behind the wreath-decorated doors with spring flowers blooming in the buckets on the front porches.

If I truly believe Jesus' death and resurrection make all the difference in my life and that He is the only true hope in this world, why am I not more intentional about sharing His love with the hurting friends and neighbors that God has placed in my life?

Easter Sunday is quickly approaching. My prayer is that I will use this week to really engage in conversation with my neighbors and offer them the hope I've experienced, which I know only comes from a relationship with Jesus. People are more likely to visit a church or any gathering where they know someone who attends. A warm and genuine invitation is often all it takes to turn someone from considering attendance to walking through the doors.

Will you join me in praying for opportunities to share with our friends and neighbors? Let's pray for that unexpected encounter at the mailbox or bus stop, for the minor inconvenience of running out of sugar, and for the courage to knock on our neighbor's door to ask if we can borrow a cup. Let's ask (and expect) God to provide an easy and natural way to connect and invite a friend to church on Sunday.

EIGHTEEN

Celebrate If We Only Knew

My daughter was not very happy. That morning, her boyfriend called to let her know the conditions were not ideal for skiing, and they needed to change their plans. Throughout breakfast with some friends, she quietly sulked while trying to hide her disappointment.

If she only knew.

During breakfast, his mother called and needed them to go by the beach house to check a leak the neighbor had noticed. While at the beach house, he thought he'd make the best of the situation and asked my daughter to walk down to the beach and skip rocks together.

She continued to pout. It was cold and rainy outside. She had no desire to be outside, let alone down by the water. She wanted to be on the ski slopes. Not at the beach house on a sopping cold and dreary day.

Oh, if she only knew.

He tried a few times to convince her to go down to the water. When she finally conceded, he walked her to the water's edge, knelt on one knee, pulled out a tiny box, and asked her to marry him.

Now, she knew.

They drove across the bay to his uncle's house, where all her sisters from out of town, along with his family and their friends, were waiting to celebrate. We joyously celebrated all weekend long.

Her big sister was genuinely happy for her and loved every minute of the festive weekend. Secretly, however, she also wanted to get engaged.

I tried to comfort her and remind her of the circumstances her boyfriend was in, as he had just accepted a new job across the country and needed to be there within a few weeks. He had yet to tell his family and had no time to think about buying a ring or asking her dad for his blessing to marry his daughter. "Give him time," I encouraged her. I assured her that within a month or so, he would be able to slow down, sort out the details, and ask her to be his wife. She understood, but I knew she was still a little sad.

If she only knew.

We took her to the airport. I kissed and hugged her and told her to keep her chin up. She landed a few hours later and drove home. It was late, and she was exhausted and needed a good night's sleep.

As she opened the door to her apartment, she became startled at what she thought was someone in her home. Sure enough, her boyfriend was there. With soft music serenading them and rose petals strewn among the dimly lit candles, he took her hand, walked her inside, knelt down on one knee, pulled out a tiny box, and asked her to marry him.

Now, she knew.

Throughout the weekend, I wondered if I was coming to understand a glimpse of how God feels when He knows "the rest of the story" and just wants His children to trust Him and believe something great is in store. At each turn of events, I wanted to whisper in their ears, "It's going to be fabulous! Trust me. I know what this weekend holds. You will be much happier with these plans than the ones you originally had."

I knew that by the weekend's end, these two daughters of mine would be engaged. As I watched their reactions to unrealized plans while privy to the bigger picture, I wanted so badly to cup their sweet faces in my hands and tell them to wait until they knew the rest of the story.

Jeremiah 29:11 reminds us that God has great plans for us, plans to prosper us and give us a future and a hope. We need to trust that His plans are better than ours. He longs to cup our sweet faces in His masterful hands and assure us that He knows and has orchestrated the rest of the story. It's going to be fabulous!

If we only knew.

NINETEEN

Celebrate Solitude

The invitation to solitude and silence is just that. It is an invitation to enter more deeply into the intimacy of relationship with the One who waits just outside the noise and busyness of our lives. It is an invitation to the adventure of spiritual transformation in the deepest places of our being, an adventure that will result in greater freedom and authenticity and surrender to God than we have yet experienced.

— RUTH HALEY BARTON

I first accepted the invitation to solitude many years ago when an article challenged me to spend five to ten minutes in silence before God each day. I would sit quietly and try to focus on the Lord. This was different from my normal prayer time because the only thing I would say at the beginning of my time was, "Lord, speak to me. Your servant is listening." Then I would be still and quiet and wait.

At times, I would hear nothing and feel as though it were a waste of time. However, over the course of a few weeks, I began to sense a need to spend quiet time alone with Him. What initially started as an act of obedience soon evolved into a longing and desire.

I remember one of the first times I was sitting quietly when I suddenly realized I could hear the ticking of the clock. It amazed me that the clock had been ticking every second of every day I had lived in that house, yet I had never noticed it. I had been too busy, my mind too cluttered, to hear the clock ticking. That day, the Lord spoke to my heart and helped me understand there were many more things I had missed because I wasn't spending time quietly listening to Him.

The discipline of solitude and silence holds utmost importance in our faith journey, yet it appears to be the least practiced. We tend to follow the world's lead in valuing doing over being. The desire to be seen, noticed, and applauded by others is not satisfied by retreating to a secluded spot and remaining still before the Lord.

Our need to actively participate, strive, and persevere often overshadows our genuine need to be still, to stop striving, and to simply sit in His presence and bask in His love. My challenge to you—and even more to myself—is to accept this invitation from our Abba Father to come before Him, sit quietly, and simply listen.

TWENTY

Celebrate Tea

I t's not just a drink—it's an experience! I adore everything about tea. Friends who say I'm an Anglophile are right. I cherish all things British. In fact, my youngest daughter's name is Britain. We tell her she's our souvenir from the three years we spent in England.

In her book, *If Teacups Could Talk*, author Emilie Barnes recounts a time when she and her granddaughter shared tea. Emilie reflected on the fact that when her granddaughter requested a tea party, what she was truly asking for was time together. Asking for tea was her way of saying, "I need to talk to you."

I began learning this lesson while living in England. Partly to stay warm and mostly to immerse myself in the culture, I embarked on my quest for knowledge and appreciation of one of life's finer pleasures: a good cup of tea. My first taste of authentic tea was at a women's gathering in a lovely garden on the High Street in St. Ives. The tea was delightful, the scones and finger sandwiches were a genuine treat, and the gardens were beautifully overgrown in that charming British way. I fell in love. I enjoyed tea with my dear British friend, Carol. My neighbor Lindsey and I shared countless cups of tea as we tackled the neighborhood issues in our small village of Brampton.

The true luxury of tea became clearer during these times, and I now fully understand my neighbor in South Carolina who invited me for coffee at her house many years ago. As excited as I was to visit her and get to know her, I felt anxious because I did not drink coffee. I worried the entire week and sheepishly walked over to her house on Friday morning. She had a lovely, simple spread on a backyard table, and guess what? She served lemonade! Her invitation was not for coffee; it was for my company.

While living in Tucson, my mentor Cynthia and I shared countless cups of tea. In other words, I needed to talk to her almost every week! We drank tea at both my house and hers. Her patio became a refuge for me; her company and words of wisdom were my rays of hope. I remember sitting at her bar, watching her boil the water and set two teacups on the tray. While observing her as she tended to the process was remarkable in itself, the experience of just the two of us sipping tea and sharing life was incredibly healing.

In almost every culture and nationality, drinking tea brings people together. It offers a necessary rhythm of slowing down and enjoying one another's company. The Lord has provided us with this wonderful way to connect with friends and neighbors, so what are you waiting for? Invite someone to tea!

TWENTY-ONE
Celebrate Tea Parties

Years ago, I started hosting tea parties at my home to connect with women in my neighborhood. Once a month, I invited neighbors, women from church, women I had been stationed with before, and even women I met at the grocery store to come and enjoy tea and each other's company. I always made sure they knew they were encouraged to invite their friends and neighbors as well. It was amazing to witness these women, who often didn't have much in common, spend a few hours connecting and discovering they truly had more in common than they had originally thought.

Three Friday morning teas stand out as the most memorable ones. The first began when my next-door neighbor, an elderly African American woman, came up my back stairs with one of the young lifeguards from our community pool in tow. She was 22 years old and working in America for the summer, as she was from the Czech Republic.

They entered the door, and my neighbor, Mildred, introduced her young friend to the rest of us. A few minutes later, I walked into the kitchen and said to her, "Here are the cups, Marita; choose any tea you'd like." She turned to me and, in her best broken English, replied, "You remembered my name? Nobody ever remembers my name."

We all had great conversations, and at the end of our time together, I asked the women to gather around a friend who was moving to Japan so we could pray for her and her family. I'm sure Marita wondered what on earth she had gotten herself into as we held hands and prayed over Lacey. After the prayer several of us continued our conversation while others got ready to leave.

When Marita and my neighbor, Mildred, prepared to leave, Marita turned to me and expressed her gratitude for allowing her to join the tea. She mentioned she had never experienced anything like it before, only having seen something similar on TV. I like to think she left that morning changed. She sensed the Lord's presence, even if she couldn't name it, and someday, she will look back on that experience in America and know that it was, indeed, the Lord.

At another memorable tea occasion, my Japanese friend from church brought her next-door neighbor, Oy, who originally hailed from Thailand. Oy, a Buddhist, was quite shy. She visited several times, always bringing her adorable young children with her. On one visit, she brought a jackfruit. I had never seen one before and was unaware of how time-consuming it could be to peel and prepare. Watching her, I honestly didn't think it was worth the effort involved. It truly was a labor of love for her.

Eventually, Oy became part of our tea group. Each month, as she attended, she engaged in numerous conversations about Jesus. She even assisted in packing my dishes when we moved.

The third memorable experience occurred while living in D.C. Most of our fellow apartment residents were millennials who worked during the day, but I knew there were a handful of women who stayed home. I sent out invitations to about ten women. Five women came to tea that morning, and it was evident they were hand-picked by God to be there.

Two ladies were original residents of the previous building that had been torn down in an attempt at gentrification. Shirley was an older woman with great-grandchildren, while Lori was about my age. Two other women came from the island of Mauritius, off the coast of Madagascar. Leelin's husband was a diplomat, and she was accompanied by a friend who was visiting. Interestingly, I learned that morning that Mauritius is home to several different nationalities who settled there.

Leelin is of Chinese descent, while her friend, who had very dark skin, is of French descent.

And then there was my friend, Nasro. Nasro is Muslim and fled many years ago from the wars and unrest in her home country of Somalia. As diverse as we all were, we had a wonderful morning full of engaging conversations. I hadn't spent much time with Nasro before, and to be honest, I didn't think we had much in common. However, as we talked and got to know each other, I discovered she has five children: four girls and one boy. We also found out that we both lived in the same town in Florida for a short time. At one point, Nasro got excited and exclaimed, "We have so much in common!" As they left, everyone agreed that we must meet again.

I often envision Mary and Elizabeth sharing tea together, eagerly awaiting the arrival of their baby boys. They dream out loud together, yet never fully comprehend how God would use their little boys in such significant and powerful ways. I like to think of Jesus enjoying many cups of tea in the homes he visited as a child and throughout his three years of public ministry. A tea party is truly a wonderful way to share God's love with people.

TWENTY-TWO
Celebrate While Suffering

Susie Larson writes, "May you lovingly dare to enter into a suffering that's not your own for the greater good of the kingdom." And she wisely adds that we must refuse "blessing guilt," that feeling of guilt because someone else is suffering while I have been blessed not to experience that particular hardship, but instead, embrace a kingdom mindset.

In today's fallen world, many areas of suffering do not directly impact us but still affect us. Another school shooting has recently claimed the precious lives of innocent children and adults. How can I connect with the survivors' devastation and grief?

A friend texted me last night to inform me that she has been diagnosed with cancer. Obviously, prayer is an essential offering, but my heart yearns for more tangible ways to support my fearful friend. Another friend recently lost her husband, and her grief has put her life on hold.

I live on a military base, and as I write, I observe methodical chaos across the street. Furniture and boxes line the driveway as they are loaded onto the moving van. People here are constantly moving. The emotions related to moving are typically bittersweet, fluctuating from excitement to fear to anxiety. Traveling down the highway to a new location means leaving friends and familiarity behind while coming to terms with loneliness and loss. What practical ways can I bring hope and comfort, I wonder?

Racial tension continues to permeate the news and specific neighborhoods. Yes, we witness progress, but we also acknowledge there is still significant work to be done. How can I support those who are suffering and truly make a difference?

People are living on the streets, children are bouncing from one foster home to another, and elderly or single neighbors are living alone and feeling lonely. Many suffer from mental illness and the societal stigma of being misunderstood.

Suffering runs rampant in our broken world. While I cannot change the world—the thought of that responsibility paralyzes me—I can ask God how I might enter into the suffering of someone He has placed within my sphere of influence. Without unnecessary and unwarranted "blessing guilt," my prayer is that God will prompt me to act on His behalf.

Perhaps I can send my friend a playlist and a prayer shawl for her chemo treatments, provide goody bags for my moving neighbors' children, invite a lonely neighbor for dinner or a movie, become a Guardian ad Litem for foster children, bring a meal to someone living on the street or in the woods, and most importantly, take time to sit and listen to the stories of those who are suffering. Everyone has a story, and most include suffering. May we bring the love of Jesus as we lovingly dare to enter in.

TWENTY-THREE

Celebrate Mother's Day

To my friends who are trying to mend the holes in their hearts from the loss of their mom, I pray today is filled with sweet memories, laughter from family jokes, awkward moments, or just plain silliness your mom unknowingly passed down to you. I pray you will feel a sense of peace and comfort as the Lord guides you through this day.

To those who long to be mothers and bravely face their fears each month, swallowing the chalice of disappointment as months turn into years, I pray that hope will be your steady companion. Perhaps, just for today, you might focus your thoughts on the One who brought you life and delight in the fact you are here.

And tomorrow, when you pick up your cup of suffering, may you have a mighty sisterhood surrounding you, storming heaven's gates on your behalf and praying ceaselessly for your heart's desire—to hear a tiny one call you Mom. Whether that desire is born from your own flesh or granted through the miracle of adoption or fostering or by coming alongside another mother who needs her child to be loved by you, I pray Jesus will be your portion and ultimately your greatest comfort. I also pray for the gift of daughters and sons in Jesus, those born to other mothers who need your motherly love and direction in their lives.

To the moms who have lost a child, whose lives will never be the same and whose ache will never disappear: I pray Jesus will hold you tightly through days like today—birthdays, anniversaries, and even ordinary days when the unexpected avalanche of sadness begs you to stay in bed and weep. I pray that memories of days gone by, including the first look into your baby's eyes and perhaps baby giggles, will remind you of the sweetness you shared. And I pray the hope of eternity will be your strength and song until you meet again.

To my friends who have inherited children through marriage, and who may face challenges in their role as a stepmother, I pray you experience a bond with your children as they come to feel like your own. I pray for peace and a supportive relationship with their birth mom, especially if that is a struggle. I pray you feel the fullness of motherhood and are truly blessed by these added gifts of grace.

To the daughters and moms who struggle to find joy in their relationships, who long to see eye-to-eye, and who would give anything for a meaningful conversation, I pray for restoration and reconciliation. I pray that walls will crumble. I pray for that first step of reaching out and perhaps many more baby steps to regaining trust and friendship. I pray today will be a new beginning for you both.

To the moms who have spent their years tirelessly rearing their children, worrying about their health and safety, cheering them on when they made the Dean's List, and lovingly disciplining them when they made poor choices, may we continue to pray fervently for each child entrusted to our care, reminding them of the Father's love and encouraging them in their endeavors. May we who are now grandmothers cherish our children's children, loving and caring for them as we pray they carry on our legacy of faith.

To those of us blessed to have our moms walking beside us—cheering us on, praying for us, sharing family history and recipes, providing good book recommendations, and telling "remember when" stories—I pray we do not take a single day for granted. Instead, let us cherish every day we wake up with our moms in our lives. I pray we will make the most of our time, seizing opportunities for visits and phone calls, sending note cards, and giving flowers. Each night before we retire, let us say thank you to Jesus once again for our mothers. (Oh, how I love my mom!)

And finally, to those who call me mom, I pray the memories we've shared will bring wrinkle-induced smiles and belly-aching laughter when you need it most. I pray you remember the travels, the road trips, the quiet times at home, the bedtime stories, and the reminder to "make good choices" when you left the house. I pray you smile when you think of your mom in the stands cheering for you, knowing she was beaming with pride regardless of how well you performed. I pray you understand the immense joy she feels seeing you successfully "adulting" with real jobs, God-chosen soulmates, your own homes to decorate as you wish, and for some of you, the gift of now being moms yourselves.

I also pray for your continued grace as I learn to be a better mom and Ammi to all of you. Know that I pray for you daily. I speak the name and peace of Jesus over you each morning when I rise. I pray you would love and serve Jesus all the days of your lives, that you would teach your children well, and you would be deeply formed in Him. How exceedingly grateful I am that you call me Mom.

TWENTY-FOUR

Celebrate Distractions

Sometimes I think I've changed and can sit in a coffee shop to work on a writing project or two. Then I give it a try and realize I haven't changed. I'm still too easily distracted from the tasks at hand. Curiosity overtakes me, and I find myself eavesdropping and wanting to join in others' conversations, which is not always a bad thing.

Many years ago, my husband and I were in a coffee shop on a Saturday morning in Tucson. I'll make the excuse that the tables were close together, but really, I was just eavesdropping. A cute young woman entered the shop and joined a young man sitting next to us. From the body language alone, you could surmise that this was a tense meeting. The conversation progressed, and although his parting words seemed amicable, we soon discovered that he had just broken up with her.

It seemed obvious to us that she knew we knew, and we began an awkward dance of figuring out our next steps. I don't remember what persuaded us other than the Holy Spirit, but we moved in. We invited her to join us, and she started to share her story. Miraculously, we became friends. She visited often, took my teenage daughters on afternoon adventures, and became part of our family.

We encouraged her as she took a new teaching job, cheered when she started dating a special young man, and praised God for His faithfulness when she announced her engagement. She is happily married to a godly man, and they are raising their two children while she continues to teach.

Today found me at a coffee shop called Simply Be. "Coffee with a cause – extending employment and internship opportunities to individuals with special needs." Two friendly staff members greeted me when I walked in. "Hi, I'm J.D., what's your name?" Tim quickly chimed in to ask if I had seen the Commanders win the football game last night. They politely took my order with a little help from a supervisor and assured me they would start on my items right away.

Once my tea and quiche had been delivered, they waited patiently and excitedly for the next customer to arrive. They introduced themselves to each one and were over the moon when a young couple entered with a toddler who waved to them, carefully entering each order into the system. Several times, they asked each other how they were doing, with J.D. offering a hug to his friend Tim while assuring him, "We're friends. This is what friends do for each other." Their supervisor chimed in to tell them what a great team they were, to which they replied with a hearty, "Thank you!"

The shop was artfully decorated, with Bible verses and prayer journals on each table. Photos of the staff, proudly wearing their aprons and hats, adorn the few rooms. The young father was meeting with another co-worker, and they were discussing marketing. I was tempted to interrupt and ask what their company is and how the marketing is working.

This coffee shop is different from many others, yet in some ways, it is the same. I accomplished very little on my to-do list, but I left with a full heart, grateful for the experience of spending a few hours in this amazing space filled with beautiful people.

"What's your name?" Tim asked as I handed him my teapot and plate. "Michele," I replied. "Oh! I have a friend from school named Michele. Thank you for coming today, and I hope you'll come back again."

"I definitely will, Tim. It's so nice to meet you and J.D." I probably won't finish everything I aim to accomplish, but I'll surely be back. I don't want to miss what God has in store for me.

TWENTY-FIVE

Celebrate Free Popsicles

So many cars whizzed by, barely slowing to the 25 MPH limit. I was discouraged, reminding myself that I had missed the group prayer before the event and hadn't even prayed for this opportunity to connect with the commuters returning home that afternoon.

With the recent passing of my mom, I found myself teetering between the desire to be social and the longing for seclusion. To be honest, I would have preferred lying on my couch. But I hid my face behind a cardboard sign that read "Free Popsicles" and waved dutifully to the passing cars. Very few pulled into the drive to cash in on the day's deal, and only a handful slowed down enough for us to toss them an icy treat as they continued on their way.

A few comments were made by the other church members regarding the number of smiles and waves received from those passing by. Even if we weren't "selling" popsicles, at least we appeared to be making people smile.

A neighbor we hadn't met approached us. We were aware of her mother's recent passing, and she and I began to talk. I offered my condolences but did not mention my own recent loss. As we continued our conversation and she discussed the grieving process for herself and her sister, I felt compelled to share that I, too, had just lost my mom. The connection was instant. We talked a few more minutes, promising to get together again. This neighbor, now a new friend, expressed her gratitude for seeing us work to bring our community together. "It really warms my heart," she added. As she walked away, I felt seen by God.

A short time later, a Ford Excursion pulled in with two wiggly children in the back seat. They live a few doors down, and we've connected a few times, but I've been praying for more conversations. This family consists of two dads and these two precious children. We had a great conversation, and as they drove away, we thanked God for another chance to connect with them.

Not too long after, a new neighbor who moved in a month ago walked by with her two giddy golden retrievers. As she approached, she commented, "I don't know how many popsicles you've given away, but I sure have seen a lot of smiles and waves!" We were grateful for the opportunity to meet her and felt a little wink from God.

Around that time, two children we had been praying would start attending church got off the school bus and came down with their mom to help pass out popsicles. They were excited to wave the signs and sample the treats, and we were delighted to have another opportunity to connect with them.

A few minutes later, I noticed my husband, the preacher, talking with a truck driver who had stopped and chatted for quite a while. I overheard their conversation about church on Sunday, with my husband inviting him to our service.

A young mom attending our women's Bible study drove through with her two boys, who eagerly awaited a chance to choose their favorite popsicle color. When I informed her of our plans to start a children's church in the fall, she expressed excitement about bringing her kids.

The popsicles were tasty, but we realized they were just an implement God used to make several meaningful connections that day. We will probably never know the rest of the stories of the smiles, waves, and impact a little rural church with free popsicles made that day. But we know God sees our tiny efforts to love our tiny community, and we celebrate the surprising ways He continues to work.

TWENTY-SIX

Celebrate Time for Adventure

A few friends and I visited another town for a women's conference. On the last morning, as we made our way to the convention center, we wandered through the charming neighborhood where we stayed, confident that our British guide (our GPS) was taking us on the fastest route to our destination. Recently, while commiserating with an unnamed daughter of mine who was (wrongly, according to her) accused of not coming to a complete stop in her neighborhood and receiving a stiff fine, I became extra cautious to follow the 25-MPH speed limit and completely stopped at each stop sign. However, as I passed by an eye-catching, beautifully painted garage door, I lost all sense of orderly driving and stopped in the middle of the road to get a closer look at this unusual art. It was breathtaking.

A few seconds went by before I realized I was blocking a jeep from pulling out of the alley on the opposite side of the road. I quickly moved forward, and as they rounded the corner, I apologized profusely with hand gestures. They rolled down their window and started to tell us "the rest of the story."

Not only was this garage painted, but there were others as well! They explained that several garages had been decorated, some by local artists, while the majority were by an artist from Venice Beach, California. At that point, I parked the car and jumped out, hoping my faithful friends would forgive my spontaneous decision and chalk it up to my addiction to impromptu experiences. Thankfully, all four doors opened, and my girlfriends followed suit splendidly.

We were awed and amazed. We strolled from one property to the next, navigating the first alley as we tried to capture with our phone cameras the beautiful flowers and vibrant images spray-painted on garage doors, side panels, and wooden fences. We spotted one across the street as the alley extended another block. With "oohs" and "aahs" and several "Look, there's another one!" we made our way up and down, reading various plaques with descriptions about the murals along the route. One responsible friend eventually convinced us that we needed to resume our journey to the convention center, so we climbed back in the car, and off we went.

The conversation continued for miles about how beautiful the paintings were, the creativity and thought that birthed each one, and the uniqueness they added to what would have been an otherwise dull alley of garage doors. Perhaps the most significant thought was how this endeavor must have brought all the neighbors together. Not only would it have required a substantial financial commitment from each home-owner, but we imagined the conversations and collaboration it must have taken to decide whose door would convey which "Be" attitude and which flower best represented each sentiment. (Be Kind; Be Celebrated; Be Curious; Be Active; Be Peace; Be Grateful; Be Bold; Be Love; Be Remembered; Be the Change; Be Joyful; Be Unforgettable, etc.)

We arrived at our conference eager to uncover more exciting glimpses of the holy. Grateful for the unexpected adventure, I appreci-ated the reminder to include margins in my schedule and to always be on the lookout for the serendipitous smiles that God loves to gift along the way.

TWENTY-SEVEN

Celebrate All Such People

While reading Corinthians recently, I came across an exhortation from Paul I didn't remember seeing before. Although the concept is prevalent in Jesus' teachings, it's one I don't always practice. As I read and reread, I became convinced this small act could significantly impact someone's day. Therefore, I asked Jesus for opportunities to intentionally emulate Paul's ways as he concluded his letter to the Corinthians: a simple admonition to "recognize such people" (1 Cor. 16:18 CSB).

In the preceding paragraph of the chapter, Paul mentioned the household of Stephanas and commended them for serving the saints. In verse 18, he continued, writing, "For they have refreshed my spirit and yours. Therefore, recognize such people." Therefore, acknowledge these individuals. There it is: the principle of recognizing those who rejuvenate and inspire us on our journey.

My first stop after reflecting on these words was the gym. On this particular day we had an instructor I had seen a few times. She was very friendly but not my type in the typical sense. Her language and lifestyle led me to believe we didn't have much in common, aside from our shared appreciation for a good workout. In fact, our reasons for being at the gym didn't even align; she loved to work out, while I grudgingly tolerated it as a necessary task to check off my day's list.

Looking past our differences, I began to notice her teaching practices. Her love of exercise was obvious. She was a great encourager to all levels of participants in her class. She made a valiant effort to learn and remember the new people's names. (This is a huge plus in my book!) And she stayed afterward to chat with us as we wiped down our sweaty equipment and gathered our belongings. She was an excellent teacher. She refreshed me, and I needed to tell her.

Instead of my usual farewell greeting of "Great class; thanks," I waited a few extra minutes and, in front of the other classmates, said to her, "Thank you. You are a great instructor! I love how you encourage all of us, and I'm grateful for you." Judging by the look on her face and the brief silence that followed, I'm pretty sure Jesus, through me, made her day. And that made mine.

So from now on, I'll be watching for more ways to "recognize all such people."

TWENTY-EIGHT

Celebrate a Time to Get Up

Reveille sounded at 6:00 a.m. this morning, calling the troops to "rise and shine." I have treasured this tradition since my early years, having lived on many military installations. I remember being about seven years old and singing along every morning, "It's time to get up, it's time to get up, it's time to get up in the morning."

The weather has been warming lately, so we had left our bedroom window open. When the bugle sounded, I sang those words in my head but then heard another voice. In my spirit, I heard the Lord say, "It's time to get up, it's time to get up, it's time to get up this morning. I have a word for you, and I need you to get up."

I second-guessed the stirring in my heart and reluctantly decided to rise and go to my chair with my Bible and journal to spend some time with the Lord. I tiptoed out of bed and quietly shut the door to avoid waking my husband and dog. In the kitchen, I made my morning tea and then headed to my chair. So far, so good.

Suddenly, I heard my husband call from the second floor, "Hey, Meg (his name for me), what are you doing? Are you coming back up?" I tried to whisper to him, "I'm getting up. I felt like the Lord was telling me to get up, that He had something for me." Hoping I'd satisfied him, I returned to the living room, and he shut the bedroom door.

I settled in with my tea and Bible and began to pray, asking God to speak to me, for I was listening. I prayed against any distractions or noises, feeling that this was a time to be silent and listen, as I'm so easily distracted. The moment I said "Amen," I heard the bedroom door open; the dog came running down the stairs, the cat began meowing incessantly, and my husband bounded down the stairs as well. (I think he was doing jumping jacks on each step.) He went into the kitchen, where he proceeded to bang pots, clank dishes, and noisily pour cat food into her dish.

I was incredibly irritated. I muttered under my breath, "You have got to be kidding me, Lord. I thought you had something for me. Do you really expect me to concentrate and listen to You when the circus is performing in the next room?"

Thankfully, I heard Him respond. "I've ordained this time together, and I'll redeem our time. Your role was to show up and listen. Thank you for your obedience."

I sat quietly for the next thirty minutes, blocking out the heavy sighing coming from the dog lying next to me and my husband singing his favorite song over and over, and just listened. I reflected on God's indescribable love for me, recounted His faithfulness in the past, but mostly I just sat still and listened. This was a discipline I had been accustomed to practicing most mornings. However, with the extra traveling I had been doing, I had not taken time to sit in silence and solitude for several months, so it felt good to "just show up."

As I concluded my time in silence, I was drawn to a book on my side table, *Invitation to Solitude and Silence* by Ruth Haley Barton. I had finished reading it several months earlier but felt compelled to open it and reread the last chapter titled, "For the Sake of Others." And there was my treasure He had waiting for me.

Several paragraphs in that chapter spoke directly to a relational situation I've been struggling with. He provided insight and the next steps I needed to take. I concluded my time with a prayer of gratitude for the wake-up call and for God's clear message, despite the interruptions.

TWENTY-NINE

Celebrate a Cold Shower

I was on my way to speak at a retreat. Friends were riding with me, and I was trying to be mindful of the time. Looking forward to a warm—no, hot—shower, I peeled off my jams, threw my towel into our towel warmer, turned on the bathroom heater, adjusted the faucet, and waited for the room to gloriously fill with steam. I waited. And waited. But the water was only lukewarm, and you know what Jesus says about being lukewarm.

Instead of watching the steam rise, I was keenly aware of the anger building within me. My first instinct was to mutter a few choice words about the injustice I was experiencing. Yes, I love Jesus, but sometimes I let a curse slip. Ask my grown children. When they first heard me, their initial shock turned to encouragement as they recognized the imperfect mom I've always been but often wished to hide from the world.

I threw on my robe and marched downstairs to interrupt my husband's quiet time, inquiring about the lack of hot water. All the while, that unsettling feeling of entitlement continued to swell within my soul. "A hot shower is not a luxury," I told myself. My husband quickly came to my aid and offered to bring hot water from the pot in the kitchen to at least wash my hair.

As he hurried down the stairs, the Spirit reminded me of my daughter, who had just returned from a three-week survey trip to Africa. She and her husband and children were planning to move there soon, and a great day for them would be having enough water, at any temperature, for one of them to take a shower.

I took a breath and refocused on gratitude for having water at all. I called down to my hubby not to bring the hot water up, and I proceeded to wash my hair and even sponge off with cold water. I reflected on all the things I'm grateful for in these moments.

Thank you, God, for shampoo and conditioner; a towel warmer (truly a luxury!); a warm towel; lotion; a comb; a bathrobe; and clean clothes. The list continued as I made my way to the bedroom to get dressed.

As I slipped on my pink tennis shoes from a closet bursting with various options, I noticed a large dog footprint in the center of my shoe. I was reminded of the weekend before when we visited friends whose ultra-friendly dog tromped through the mud to greet me. Rather than feeling annoyed, I was filled with joy from fond memories and a grateful heart for a generous friend who shares her farm, food, family, and dog with us. I packed my bags for the weekend, thanking God for all He has given me, especially for a cold shower.

THIRTY

Celebrate What You Do

On a trip to visit our dear British friends Bob and Carol, I was struck by the sentiment Bob dutifully exclaimed each time he walked Carol to the door as she left the house. Regardless of where she was headed—whether to shop for meal ingredients, visit a friend, hop on a bus, or spend the day volunteering at a local school—he always sent her off with the admonition to "Love what you do." (In his perfect British accent, no less!)

But it got me thinking. What if we made a conscious decision to love everything we did? As we traveled to work, whether an anticipatory drive or a dreadful one, what if we asked Jesus to help us love what He has called us to do?

As we visit a neighbor or dedicate our time to help those in need, when we respond to uninvited interruptions in our day, when fearful situations demand our presence, when menial tasks must be accomplished, oh Jesus, help us to love what we do.

As I head out the door each morning, may I unlock the key to the opportunities set before me with a mindset to love what I do. Whatever Jesus has in store for me, I pray I will hear His gentle reminder, in His reassuring fatherly (perhaps British?) voice, to go out into the day and "Love what you do."

Celebrate All Work as Sacred

With today being Labor Day, the topic of yesterday's sermon at our church was aptly titled "The Sacredness of Work." I followed along fairly studiously; however, I tend to miss a thought or two, mostly due to being distracted by the attractive preacher delivering the message. Please don't worry; my husband is aware of my struggle in this area, although he's not sure he wants me to overcome this challenge.

He referred to Genesis 1:26, where man's first work assignment was to "rule the fish of the sea, the birds of the sky, the livestock, the whole earth, and the creatures that crawl on the earth" (CSB). The text goes on to remind us of God's directive to care for the land and, ultimately, to care for each other. What resonated with me the most, however, was God's example as He fulfilled His work. After God created everything, Genesis 2:2 states, "On the seventh day God had completed His work that He had done, and He rested on the seventh day from all His work that He had done. God blessed the seventh day and declared it holy, for on it He rested from all His work of creation" (CSB).

These few verses remind us of the importance of both working and resting. Later in the New Testament, Paul encourages us by saying, "Whatever you do, do it from the heart, as something done for the Lord and not for people, knowing that you will receive the reward of an inheritance from the Lord" (Col. 3:23–24 CSB). This serves as a significant reminder that regardless of the nature of our work, there is value and sacredness in doing our best.

I recently succumbed to the dreaded visit to the DMV to surrender my Florida driver's license and begin life as an official resident of Virginia. Part of my trepidation regarding this process was the actual trip to the DMV. Ironically, I had just heard a song on the radio dissing this establishment and portraying it as a place we all loathe. I went prepared to be turned away, surely not having brought whatever specific documents they required.

I made an appointment and brought a book to pass the time during my long wait. Surprisingly, there was no one in line ahead of me. Even more surprising was the warm and friendly smile I received along with the greeting, "Hello, how can I help you?" Clutching my life history in a brown manila envelope, I spread all my papers on the counter and somehow managed to bring everything I needed. As I waited for the clerk to find me in the database, I noticed her shirt that read, "There is power in the name of Jesus!" She proceeded to process my request as efficiently as the computer would allow. She was kind. She was friendly. And so were her co-workers. This was not the DMV experience we expected.

As I left a few minutes later, I wondered if the difference was that she valued work. She understood all jobs to be sacred and worthy of being done well. She was working for the Lord, looking forward to her reward: an inheritance from Him. Oh, that we would all execute our work as a sacred gift offered to the Lord.

THIRTY-TWO

Celebrate the Garden of Gethsemane

A fter I returned from a pilgrimage to Israel, many people asked about the highlights of my journey. Several memories came to mind, but the one that kept surfacing was the Garden of Gethsemane.

I visited this beautiful space a few years ago on my first Holy Land trip, but the experience this time was different. My initial visit was more of a personal excursion, as I reflected on the events that occurred and how they impacted me. Unfortunately, since it was all about me, I missed out on an important gift: the opportunity to see the Garden through the perspective of a connected community.

The insightful book, *Misreading Scripture with Western Eyes*, showed me our default thinking in Western, particularly North American, culture is often overly centered on individualism. We misinterpret Scripture when we confuse its application with its meaning. The meaning of John 3:16, for instance, clearly states, "For God so loved the world." While we may apply this truth to our lives, its true meaning encompasses a love for the entire world, indicating that all who believe in Him will not perish. It is a communal truth, yet we frequently read it with an individual perspective in mind.

Considering what a certain passage means to me involves two careful paths: the first is the assumption that all Scripture is intended for me individually, and the second is the belief that if a passage doesn't resonate with my personal circumstances, it lacks relevance. It is a cultural phenomenon that seeks to interpret Scripture from a personal perspective. In Jesus' time and culture, community and collective thought were considered more valuable than individual understanding.

Certainly, there are times to read Scripture for personal insight and answers, and yes, there are times when Scripture is intended solely for us as individuals. However, as I continue to read and listen to Jesus every day, I'm excited to embrace new perspectives, such as reading to discover God's character and for the collective community.

Which brings me back to the Garden. During my most recent visit to the Garden of Gethsemane, I experienced the fullness of community within the Garden. An older gentleman was visibly moved and began weeping as a small group of believers sang the chorus, "Were You There When They Crucified My Lord?"

Several women were seated on rocks or benches throughout the Garden, holding tightly to their rosaries as they prayed. A young man was penning his thoughts in a leather-bound journal, contemplating the significance around him. Fellow pilgrims focused intently on the olive trees, the lavender bushes, and the creative beauty of the sacred, stopping to reflect, to wonder, and to capture moments to carry with them. We were all personally experiencing Jesus in the Garden, yet together as well.

Reading Scripture and finding Jesus in our daily lives through the lens of community brings about a rich awareness that it's not all about me. I am but a tiny speck in God's masterfully created redemptive plan. This outlook can bring a sense of togetherness and kinship, as well as a responsibility to remember that we are all in this divinely chosen life together. As I acknowledge and treasure my personal relationship with Jesus, these days, I am equally excited to focus on the bigger picture, which includes the world that God so loved.

THIRTY-THREE

Celebrate Prayer—Not Just Talking to God

A fter moving to a new community, I met a fellow military spouse whom I had previously heard about and was excited to get to know. During our initial conversation, she shared details about herself and her family, as well as more about her experiences. By the end of our twenty-minute chat, I had learned quite a bit about her, yet she knew nothing about me.

Our one-sided "conversation" reminded me of how often my dialogues with God unfold in a similar manner. I used to spend my entire prayer time talking, missing the chance to listen and learn, understand Him on a deeper level, and marvel as He reveals His attributes and characteristics.

Having attended prayer workshops and read books on the subject, I am struck by the revelation of how often we overlook the most important aspect of prayer: listening. We teach various methods, including the ACTS acronym (Adoration, Confession of our sins, Thanksgiving, and Supplication). Yet in each of these components, we are the ones who speak. Granted, these practices are all noble and necessary for our relationship with Jesus; however, the invitation to be still and listen to Him speak becomes lost in our attempts to tell Him everything He already knows.

As in our earthly relationships, we must listen to God more than we speak if we truly desire to know Him. Several things might hinder this discipline; our human nature often feels uncomfortable with silence, or perhaps we fear what God may reveal to us during those quiet moments. Practicing this discipline requires patience and effort. Our minds tend to wander, but God longs to communicate with us. As we engage in our prayer times, may we strive to be still and ask God what He wishes to share with us. Then, let us take the opportunity to sit and listen. We know He will speak to us.

THIRTY-FOUR
Celebrate Loving and Listening Well

I've heard it said that loving others well is a sign of spiritual maturity. I would argue that it is the definitive sign of spiritual maturity. I can hardly think of another attribute that compares. Knowledge, education, experience, empathy, and compassion are all admirable qualities; however, they fall short of following Jesus' two greatest commandments to "Love the Lord your God with all your heart, all your soul, and all your mind" and, equally important, to "Love your neighbor as yourself" (Matt. 22:37,39). In fact, perhaps the true sign of loving God well is, indeed, loving others well.

I've been asking God to teach me how to love others well, and I first recognized a shift in my perspective in a recent meeting. As we circled the table sharing prayer requests, one person began to explain their concern. Rather than providing a quick overview, they continued for several minutes expounding on what I considered unnecessary details. Half-heartedly paying attention while concentrating on other matters of the day, I noticed others sharing my sentiment of boredom and the desire to move the conversation along. Suddenly, my mind began to process the scenario through a different lens—Jesus' lens.

Instead of selfishly biding my time and waiting to move on to more important topics, I allowed my curiosity to take over and recalled previous conversations with this person, remembering that she often processes her thoughts aloud. Rather than assuming she wanted to be seen as the important, informed one who knows all the details of the situation, I started to wonder if this person was simply sharing her thoughts with all of us as a way of processing them for herself. Perhaps she just needed someone to listen so that she could better grasp the situation and understand it personally.

It's only been a few days, but I've begun to view other conversations through a new perspective—Jesus' perspective. Loving well involves listening well. And because we, as Christians, aspire to be like Jesus, we should strive to become better listeners, both to Jesus and to each other.

THIRTY-FIVE

Celebrate the Power of One

S everal years ago, when our family moved to a new area, we began the intimidating task of "church dating". After visiting at least seven churches, we felt led to join a particular one. Even though it was the largest one we tried, we all agreed it was the friendliest.

After taking time to think through our decision to attend this church, it dawned on me that, really, it came down to one person who went out of her way to make us feel welcomed and connected.

That same year, the Grand Finale of Husfelt High School Graduations had just commenced. I had to confess that during those last few weeks of having a child in school, I said a few times how happy I was to be finished dealing with high schools. (This being our fifth one.) Sitting through the ceremony, I noticed one of the counselors from the school whom we'd had a particularly difficult time with that year. After taking time to think through my feelings, it dawned on me that really, it was just that one staff person who soured my outlook on high schools in general, and this one especially.

The Power of One.

Comparing these two experiences, I was reminded that it only takes one person to make a place seem fabulous or faltering. The church was very friendly, but it really started with just one person who made it seem like the whole church was friendly. High Schools are horrible places. No, not necessarily. It really was just one high school counselor who made it seem that way.

I have seen The Power of One. And I want to be that One. I want to be the One who takes a step out of my comfort zone and speaks to new people. I want to be the One who stays a few extra minutes and connects with someone who needs encouragement. I want to be the One who allows my schedule to be interrupted so that someone else feels important and valued. I want to be the One God uses to comfort another, walking alongside someone who is struggling, igniting a spark of Hope in someone who is experiencing hopelessness. I want to be the one who brings glory to God and speaks His peace to those He places in my path. "Lord, help me to be more concerned with those around me than I am with my needs, my comfort, and my schedule. Help me to love deeply with the love that comes only from You. Amen"

THIRTY-SIX
Celebrate As We Pay Attention

Our fall writer's retreat has begun. Starting with breakfast featuring Michele B.'s famous quiche, made with fresh eggs from her happy chicks, we moved into the quaint sanctuary of Mt. Pisgah Baptist Church, a historically Black church on the outskirts of Upperville.

The foyer is adorned with pictures and portraits of the faithful men whose legacy lives on within these walls. A tambourine rests in the fourth pew, anticipating the next worship service and the opportunity to sing its praises to the creator and sustainer of all things. Banners proclaim the names of the Father and the admonition to be still. The smell of antique oak fills the air, paired with the thought of all the trees that sacrificed their branches to adorn this sacred space. If only they could talk...

Katie and Carrie are walking together down the road leading to the village. Amanda is ahead, perhaps intent on listening to God as she makes her way to the outdoor sanctuary behind Trinity Church. Jackie is sitting on the front stoop of Mt. Pisgah, admiring the many shades of green while pondering the question, "Is green perhaps God's favorite color?" As she recalls her recent visit to Colombia, her phone rings with a call from a Colombian friend.

Paula is set up in the fellowship hall, with her computer and journal in hand. Adria is taking in the sight of a baby deer and the cacophony of sounds as she sits in the gazebo behind the church, surrounded by the farm next door. And I am observing it all from the front porch of the pastorium—though not alone, as Hazel Grace (the Goldendoodle) has been waiting for a morning companion. For me, seeing others connect with God and each other is a spiritual high. In these ordinary and mostly mundane places, God is working among us in extraordinary ways.

At 12:30, we gather back, load up the cars, and head to the Locke Store to buy lunch and pay attention. We then divert for a quick jaunt into Paris, where we admire the different homes and roll our windows down to talk to John. He is cleaning out his stone house and will tell us more when we have "cocktails." (He is our neighbor and friend.) He offers advice on ordering sandwiches at the Locke Store and sends us on our way.

As we enter Millwood, we park at the Mill and collect our chairs and picnic blankets to deposit beside the running stream, which beckons us to come and sit for a spell. We join several others inside to select our sandwiches and various sundries, perusing the gourmet food displays, which invite us to indulge a little more than usual on this Saturday afternoon.

Back at our picnic spot, we sit, stand, and splash in the stream, and we chat with fellow picnickers. We pass around bread lathered with lemon hummus, an informal yet perhaps overlooked reminder that we partake in a piece of the eucharist each time we break bread together. We savor this time of community.

Satisfied yet yearning for more, we return to Mt. Pisgah and remain vigilant. The main topic of discussion revolves around the consensus that our time has once again been too brief. "It takes a few hours to unwind and embrace the quiet stillness," one writer reflects. "And we have so much to share with one another when we can connect face-to-face," another remarks. We all agree we need another day.

In the last hour, we break away to spread out and listen individually. God continues to reveal His goodness, and we, as scribes, faithfully pen

His thoughts. As the end of our day draws nigh, we gather once again in community, circling our seats to hear from one another. We all partake by sharing and listening, with celebration and affirmation. The Lord has spoken. This is holy ground.

THIRTY-SEVEN

Celebrate Our Royalty

W e all knew it was inevitable. Even royalty is not immune to God's design for our lives. We learned this lesson firsthand while living in England in 1997, when we woke up to the shocking news that Princess Diana had been killed. We joined thousands of others in front of Kensington Palace, feeling the loss despite being recent transplants to the Motherland.

During our brief three-year stay, we immersed ourselves in the culture and community of the U.K. We learned to appreciate the narrow village lanes and how to back up to let lorries pass. Our children donned plasters, participated in playgroups, and attended infant and junior schools. We celebrated Guy Fawkes Day, Coronation Day, and the Queen's Golden Jubilee, during which we stood for hours in anticipation of the procession and the opportunity to see and wave to Her Majesty. It was magical. We spent Boxing Day with the village vicar and his wife, feasting on roast beef and Yorkshire pudding, enjoying a leisurely walk through the fields, and ending our day with a bowl of spotted dick, which the kids still find hilarious.

I became a tea connoisseur, righteously judging those who attempt to serve an afternoon tea blend in the morning or vice versa. We toured many castles and reveled in the history of the royal family. When our time sadly came to an end, we returned to the States with a house full of English antiques, teapots, Dorling Kindersley books, Spode, Portmeirion, and our favorite souvenir, our newest daughter, Britain Amanda-Rose. When my husband asks what kind of car I'd like next, I always reply, "A Range Rover, just like the Queen's!" (And he always chuckles.)

We loved our time in England. And we love all things British.

Though we mourned the recent death of Queen Elizabeth II and all the goodness and grace she represented, we are also reminded that we, too, are royalty. We are royal heirs, alongside the Queen of England. According to 1 Peter 2:9, we are "a chosen race, a royal priesthood, a holy nation, a people for His own possession" (ESV). Like Queen Elizabeth, we are joint heirs with Christ.

Her Majesty Queen Elizabeth was both elegant and eloquent. She exemplified the fruit of the Spirit in her life as she fulfilled her royal duties, and I assume she carried these virtues into her personal life as well. She was a remarkable soul who left behind a legacy worthy of her country and her Savior. May she be welcomed into eternity as Jesus bids her, "Well done, good and faithful servant." And may we all continue with the same hope. Now off to find my marmalade sandwich.

THIRTY-EIGHT

Celebrate Our Similarities

I n a few days, it's election day. I've come to dread the whole process. It is no longer an exciting time when we, as Americans, can cast our votes, safely voice our opinions, and then unite, regardless of who wins. Apart from a miracle, which is our hope, we brace for the divisiveness and ugly rhetoric that will spew from both sides—the name-calling, the judgment-casting, and the dissension that seems inevitable to descend as darkness on us all.

I'm also grappling with a personal relationship that, on the surface, seems to demand I take sides. I care for this friend deeply, yet differences continue to arise. Left to my own sinful ways, I might conclude it's not worth navigating the conflict. It could be easier to walk away. However, walking away wouldn't be an act of love. When we remain and live together in unity, despite our differences, we demonstrate our love for Jesus to a watching world—and a cherished friend.

Jesus urges me to remain. "Continue the work of unity," I hear Him whisper. "It is my way, and it will be worth it. There is blessing in unity." In Psalm 133:1-3, David writes, "How good and pleasant it is when God's people live together in unity! It is like precious oil poured on the head, running down on the beard, running down on Aaron's beard, down on the collar of his robe. It is as if the dew of Hermon were falling on Mount Zion. For there the LORD bestows his blessing, even life forevermore" (NIV).

According to Matthew Henry's commentary, the oil used for anointing was holy and "made up by a divine dispensatory; God appointed the ingredients and the quantities."[1] Therefore, David reminds us that unity is holy, something God has appointed, and unity among His people is precious to Him.

Unity does not require all parties to agree on issues or even concede that the others' opinions might be correct. In some instances, we may conclude that the other party has lost all common sense and is off their rocker. That's okay. We can still find common ground, especially as believers, because we are united in Christ. The blessing comes when we focus on what unites us. We must unite, not because of our similarities or differences, but because of what God has done.

As Jonathan Robbins, lead pastor at The Summit Church in Oak Ridge, North Carolina, recently preached, "We cannot separate our relationship with others from our relationship with God. We express our love for God through the way we love others." Robbins also pointed out two of the things God requires of us in Micah 6:8 relate to our interactions with each other, while only one pertains to our relationship with Him: "He has shown you, O man, what is good. And what does the Lord require of you? To act justly, to love mercy, and to walk humbly with your God" (RSV).

Often, our differences shout loudly, while our similarities softly whisper. My prayer is that I (and we) will seek to drown out the shouting and focus on the still small voice, who whispers the blessing of unity to all who hear.

---

1. https://biblehub.com/commentaries/mhc/

THIRTY-NINE

Celebrate When Love Wins

Over and over again in the past few years, the turmoil of racial injustice has swept through our masked, distant, and socially deprived nation. In the days and weeks that followed each instance, I continued to sit and listen to God, asking Him to guide my next steps.

Then this morning during my devotional, I encountered these thoughts from Mother Teresa: "I never look at the masses as my responsibility. I focus only on the individual. I can love only one person at a time. I can feed only one person at a time. Just one, one, one. You get closer to Christ by coming closer to each other."

One person at a time.

When I see the masses, I feel easily discouraged. What can I do to alleviate the issue? It seems so vast, and I am so small—a tiny drop in a massive ocean.

I tend to be mathematically challenged. Equations, constants, and coefficients never made much sense to me. Sometimes, God's use of math doesn't make much sense in human terms, but He makes up for it exponentially in eternal dividends.

And He asks us to love one person at a time. Because when they experience love, they, in turn, love another. And they another. And they another. All the tiny drops collectively begin to make a little wave. God moves among the small waves and joins them with others to make larger waves that crash against fear and hate, self-righteousness, and divisiveness.

Just because we loved one person at a time.

FORTY

Celebrate a Time to Behold

Behold. It's a word we don't often use or hear these days. In just a few days, this word has come to my attention several times, and I finally decided to sit with it to see if there was something more to this obscure compound word. As a geeky writer and editor, I often find myself dissecting words to uncover hidden treasures among syllables and sequences of letters. Staring at *behold*, I separated it into two words—*be* and *hold*—both of which invite us to pause, wait, and reflect.

I recently listened to a podcast featuring a conversation with John Mark Comer, the founder of *Practicing the Way, a pathway for apprenticeship to Jesus.* When faced with the daunting task of defining the path to becoming like Jesus in a single word, John Mark chose the word *contemplate.* A few definitions of contemplate are: "to consider one particular thing for a long time in a serious and quiet way," "to view or consider with continued attention: meditate on," and "to look at or view with continued attention; observe or study thoughtfully."[1]

"We tend to overestimate willpower and insight's ability to change

---

1. Definitions taken from Dictionary.com, Merriam-Webster.com, and Dictionary.Cambridge.org.

us," observed John Mark. "The point is you become like whatever you regularly focus on." John Mark referred to Paul's writing in 2 Corinthians 3:18 as his "one-sentence view of spiritual formation": "And we all, who with unveiled faces contemplate the Lord's glory, are being transformed into His image with ever-increasing glory" (NIV). The Greek word for contemplate is *katatēso*, which translates, "to gaze or look deeply at."

"One of the words for contemplation used by previous generations," John Mark explained, "was this word, *beholding*, which served as another English translation of Paul's language in 2 Corinthians. Earlier generations would speak of beholding prayer, gazing at God and the wonder of who He is. The pathway to becoming like God involves looking at Him," John Mark concluded.

As we enter the season of Advent, my prayer is to behold the wonder of it all. I want to slow down and meditate on the story of Jesus' birth; I want to gaze upon the brightness of the lights, the beauty of the decorations, and the people God places in my path. I want to sit and savor the silence as I listen for God's gentle whispers throughout the day. I long to be. And I long to hold on to all He has to show me. I long to behold the God who sent His only Son so many years ago and who continues to send His love in the beauty of today.

FORTY-ONE

Celebrate When the Stockings Are Hung, But They're Not Coming Home

Last Christmas Eve it was rather quiet. I reminisced about days gone by, when we seldom had a peaceful night. The chaos of five kids within eight years brought liveliness and constant chatter, much to the dismay of the eldest child, our only son, condemned to a life with four talkative little sisters.

We managed to be together for most Christmases while they were growing up. However, even then, there were a few years when their dad was away during the holidays, serving soldiers and airmen in harm's way, far from home. Christmas arrived, and the celebration continued, even though we weren't all together at home.

Fast forward through the many holidays spent in new places and homes (eighteen with children in tow), and one by one, they all headed off to college. Thankfully, they returned home for Christmas each year.

Christmas Eves continued with the traditional candlelight service and a birthday cake for Jesus, culminating in everyone opening one gift (usually pajamas). All five adult children would revert to childhood and leave their stockings outside the door of the one bedroom where they all slept together, anticipating Santa to fill their stockings by morning. At least one child would wake early and start unwrapping their stocking gifts in the dark, nudging the others to awaken and join in the thrill of guessing each gift by feeling the shape or rattling the contents. (At least one has been known to slug the sibling who dared to wake her before her time.) Oh, the joy of having them all home for Christmas!

After college graduations, they still managed to come home for a few years. But then came the weddings, sharing holidays with in-laws, and having babies who, understandably, make it difficult to travel during the holidays. They now live thousands of miles away, some even as far as Africa. All are joyous milestones, but now they don't all come home for Christmas.

Yet the celebration continues. The hours spent unwrapping gifts on Christmas morning in years past are now replaced with video calls throughout the day, with worn-out parents and excited grands demonstrating their new toys and exclaiming, "Happy Birthday, Jesus!"

We begin the morning in the usual way: Colleen's coffee cake along with tea and coffee. We met Colleen at our first military duty station in South Carolina, and we've made her Poor Man's Coffee Cake every Christmas morning since 1994. We read our Advent devotions by the tree and candlelight. We bask in the love of a baby boy who transforms us in such profound ways. We read, ponder, and wonder. We pray for our children in Africa, who delight in the opportunity to visit their neighbors, most of whom have never heard of Jesus, our Messiah, and share stories from Christ's birth.

Although our home no longer rings with the chaos and laughter of siblings and best friends unwrapping gifts and wrestling on the living room floor, we give great thanks for the memories of years gone by. We remember the bikes, basketball hoops, and doll beds assembled after everyone had gone to bed, and the five funny kids excitedly perched at the top of the stairs, waiting with great anticipation for Mom and Dad to get their tea and coffee, set up the video camera, and give the go-ahead to tumble down the stairs to see what Santa brought.

Fond memories make for warm Christmas mornings when the children don't come home. The joyful celebration of the birth of our Savior holds us together, though we are miles apart. The promise of the next generation leads us into a hope-filled new year. As our children teach their children the truth and traditions of this season, we rejoice in the Father's faithfulness to our family.

"Mama, did you know Jesus was born with no shoes and no socks and NO BLANKIES," two-year-old Hannah Jo explains to my daughter. That's right, Hannah. Because He loved us so. And though we are miles apart this Christmas, we thank God we can still rejoice together.

FORTY-TWO

Celebrate Immanuel—A Mystery to Behold

Every year during Advent, I am reminded of the name of Jesus, which assures us He is always with us. Each year, I vow to carry the name and its reality into the new year, being careful not to pack it away with the other decorations and holiday "terms." Yet somehow, I seem to lose this most transformational thought as the months scurry by and the pages of my calendar flip away the days.

Immanuel—God with us. It is indeed a mystery. Genesis informs us that Jesus, along with God and the Holy Spirit, existed before time, preceding the creation of the world. Then God said, "Let us make mankind in our image, in our likeness" (Gen. 1:26 NIV). The triune community has always existed. John further discusses the Trinity and challenges our concept of time in John 1:1–3: "In the beginning was the Word, and the Word was with God, and the Word was God. He was with God in the beginning. All things were created through him, and apart from him not one thing was created that has been created" (CSB).

In the fullness of time, when the world needed Him most, Jesus was born in the flesh, becoming a physical representation of God with us. A mysterious way to save the world, indeed. Deity transformed into humanity, taking on all human characteristics: feelings and emotions, bruised knees, dusty feet, hunger, and thirst, yet without sin. He held a special place in His heart for His mother and possessed an innate yearning for community. Jesus fully engaged in life with those around Him; He laughed, He cried, and He felt great compassion for others. He represented God the Father, embodying God with us.

As we celebrate His physical birth and await His second coming, let us not forget that He remains *Immanuel*—God with us. He is ever-present, a help in times of trouble, a celebrator, and the giver of all things good. His presence is His greatest gift. Though a mystery to our finite minds, He is still *Immanuel*—God with us.

FORTY-THREE

Celebrate the Short Days of Winter

As I write, the morning has not quite broken. The twinkling porch lights peek into my windows, and the two flames of the candle I've lit dance together in harmony. Before the chaos of the day begins, the stillness quietly beckons me to sit with Jesus and savor the moment.

The winter evenings are upon us as I make my way home from the office in the dusk. I am in awe as I pass farms with illuminated barns and silhouetted silos, framed by fences forming tidy boundaries that follow the winding roads. Horses don their winter coats, and deer dart onto the road without warning.

I love winter. I love the short days that invite me to cease my striving earlier and enjoy a few more hours reading by the fireplace with a cup of my favorite tea, a scented candle flickering about, a FaceTime call with the grands, or simple conversation with friends and family.

Snow has not yet fallen, but anticipation is building. The white snowflakes will drift down from the sky, collecting on unsuspecting objects, creating a glorious scene. Snow days offer another gift to slow down and enjoy a break from the usual hustle and bustle. I love the snow.

Fewer sunlit hours remind me of our days in Norway. The sun

would halfheartedly rise at about 10:00 a.m. and go to bed around 3:00 p.m. The children rode the bus to and from school in the dark. Every home displayed candles in the windows, while smoke billowed from the chimneys. In stark contrast to the summer nights when neighbors would mow their lawns at midnight (because the sun was still shining), the lack of sunlight provided a natural rhythm of slowing down.

As God so often does, He uses His creation of winter days to benefit us. He invites us to adjust our gait from a gallop to a two-step trot, to cozy up and enjoy the candlelit reminder of the light that shines in the darkness, the hope that emerges through the stillness, and the love of Jesus to entice us to slow down.

FORTY-FOUR

Celebrate Real People Who Deserve to Be Seen

A s I pulled up to the red light, I fumbled for my bag and rummaged through it blindly for a few dollars. I smiled as I lowered my window and waited for him to approach my car. Some dread that awkward moment, but I view it as an opportunity to brighten someone's day.

Sometimes the signs are humorous, like "Give me a dollar and I'll vote for Trump," while others tug at my heartstrings, such as "Homeless vet" or "Single mom trying to feed my children." On this day, the man's sign read, "God bless you." Regardless of the sign's message, I usually try to give something, and his sign that day confirmed my intentions.

While there are many ways to share kindness and the love of Jesus, this is just one approach I've discovered and the reasons I feel compelled to give to panhandlers:

Jesus commands it. Matthew 5:42 reminds us to "Give to the one who asks you, and do not turn away from the one who wants to borrow from you" (CSB). Jesus doesn't issue a disclaimer about giving to those who are worthy, attend church, or spend their money wisely. Thankfully, He doesn't hold us responsible for how the money we give is spent. One idea is to carry fast-food gift cards to distribute, but whatever we give, it's important to do so cheerfully.

These men and women who panhandle unknowingly provide a valuable service. They are a visible reminder of many others who are marginalized and struggling to make ends meet. They represent individuals in our society who face mental or physical challenges, and we have the great privilege through our small acts of kindness to add hope to their day. (I personally have several homeless friends and pray that someone else is helping them, as well.)

We can give from a grateful heart that humbly understands we could be standing in their place. Yes, some have made poor choices which have led them to street corners, but others have endured hardships that dictated circumstances beyond their control. As the old proverb goes, "There, but for the grace of God, go I."

Everyone has a story. Although time is often of the essence, taking a moment to listen to a piece of their story allows them to feel valued and recognize that their story matters. Simply looking them in the eyes and acknowledging their humanity brings more hope than we can imagine. We all long to be seen and heard. In my experience, no one has ever struggled to find words when asked how to pray for them.

I have a fifth, and I admit it's rather self-serving, but in my desire to be authentic, I'll share. Giving to others makes me feel good, and Proverbs 11:25 validates this, "Those who refresh others will themselves be refreshed." There are so many ways to bless others. My prayer is that you'll discover the ones that are right for you.

And next time you pull up to a red light or pass a panhandler in the metro, whether you feel led to give or not, remember to smile and acknowledge these men and women, showing some extra kindness to brighten someone else's day.

FORTY-FIVE

Celebrate the Last Ten Minutes

Halfway through my workout class, the instructor made a comment she'd never made before. To keep us on track, she remarked that the last repetitions of our current weight-lifting track were the most important.

Between wiping sweat—something I don't usually do—and finishing my reps, I replayed her words in my mind. The last repetitions are the most crucial. Toward the end of class, she explained why those final ten minutes were so important. She stated that the end of the exercise is when the muscles are most fatigued, and the easiest option is to simply give up. The initial phase involves maintaining effort, using muscles comfortably without much resistance. However, as you progress and your body becomes exhausted, your muscles enter the transformation stage. During those last few minutes, when they feel tired and the struggle is real, this is when the muscles grow stronger, and change occurs.

Because my mind is always searching for spiritual meaning in the everyday nuances around me, and perhaps because I have realized most of the people I live with are half my age, this comment from the gym coach struck me as profound wisdom for my current situation. In whatever situation I find myself, the last few minutes are the most important.

My husband and I are in a delightful stage of life. We have adult children; some are rewarding us with grandchildren, and others are including us in meaningful conversations about life decisions. We're mindful that we're approaching the last ten minutes. In my reading this morning, I came across these verses in Psalm 71:17–18: "Since my youth, O God, you have taught me, and to this day I declare your marvelous deeds. Even when I am old and gray, do not forsake me, O God, till I declare your power to the next generation, your might to all who are to come" (NIV).

We've been parenting and mentoring for a long time. Some days, exhaustion and fatigue set in, making slowing down seem quite attractive. Retiring and simply enjoying ourselves are themes our culture suggests we deserve. We've worked hard and long, and it's finally our time to relax—so we've been told. But God is reminding us that these may be the most important times. We must not slow down or give in; transition is coming, and our lives are gaining strength.

The lyrics of a song written by Steve Green and sung at our wedding remain our prayer for today: "Oh, may all who come behind us find us faithful."[1]

---

1. Green, Steve. "Find Us Faithful." Track 5 on *People Need the Lord*. 1994.

FORTY-SIX

Celebrate While Building the Kingdom

During a visit last fall to my daughter's house, I walked through her neighborhood each day, noticing several homes under construction. Over the three weeks, I observed the different stages of progress and the many crews working under the blazing Arizona sun. I was struck by the fact I never saw anyone working on a house alone; there were always at least two people on each task. I also noticed that different crews handled different jobs. Every day, there would be roofers, solar panel installers, landscapers, drywall specialists, plumbers, framers, masons, and electricians—each with specific areas they were responsible for. Despite their different roles, they all shared a common goal. Yet, no one worked alone.

I walk through each day, noticing God's Kingdom being built. Over time, I have observed the various stages of progress and the numerous crews working here on Earth. Scripture makes it clear that the Kingdom will not be built by individual workers alone, but by those working together.

Paul reminds us that, "...as in one body we have many members, and the members do not all have the same function, so we, though many, are one body in Christ, and individually members one of another. Having gifts that differ according to the grace given to us, let us use them: if prophecy, in proportion to our faith; if service, in our serving; the one who teaches, in his teaching; the one who exhorts, in his exhortation; the one who contributes, in generosity; the one who leads, with zeal; the one who does acts of mercy, with cheerfulness (Romans 12.4-8). Together, we are the body of Christ. Together, we work to build God's kingdom here on earth.

As we labor out of the strengths and gifts the Spirit has given each of us, building on the foundation of Jesus Christ, the Body is solidly built. In connecting with one another, intentionally committing to the community of believers in which we find ourselves, our work will reap great rewards. Together, we can accomplish much. Apart and alone, we feebly attempt to lay one measly brick at a time.

I'm sure there are construction workers who really are jacks of all trades. But I imagine they possess a particular skill or two for which they are more naturally equipped. And I suppose they understand the value of using their skills alongside others who are invested in the same end goal. Let's ask the Spirit to reveal to us the special gifts God has graced us with, and together with our community, discover where God is working and join Him in His work. Let's seek to uncover what the Master Builder is creating and experience the excitement and joy of being workers together until His kingdom comes. On earth as it is in heaven.

FORTY-SEVEN

Celebrate Armor That Fits

We have countless photos and memories of our young children dressing up in "big people's clothes." They particularly adored my husband's combat boots. He would come home in the evening, sit in a chair, and remove his boots. Inevitably, a few minutes later, one of the kids would be spotted attempting to walk around in those enormous boots. They never got very far but were always eager for the challenge. Occasionally, they would try on his entire uniform. Oh, how they wanted to be just like their daddy.

Our youngest daughter, Britain, was well-known among my friends as an early lover of high heels. She especially loved visiting our friend Lee in Norway, who granted Britain access to her well-stocked closet filled with fashionable heels and boots. The boots were longer than her legs, yet she would strut around the house until she fell, her feet and ankles weary from the strain of wearing shoes that didn't fit. At four years old, she was determined to be a fashion statement, just like Ms. Lee.

In the book of 1 Samuel, we encounter the well-known story of David and Goliath. David, a young and inexperienced shepherd boy, volunteered to confront the giant Goliath. I can imagine Saul muttering, "Seems rather foolish," under his breath. Nevertheless, he agreed to this absurd move and began preparing David for the mismatched contest.

"Then Saul dressed David in his own tunic. He put a coat of armor on him and a bronze helmet on his head. David fastened his sword over the tunic and tried walking around, but he was not accustomed to them. 'I cannot go in these,' he said to Saul, 'because I am not used to them.' So he took them off. Then took his staff in his hand, chose five smooth stones from the stream, put them in the pouch of his shepherd's bag, and, with his sling in hand, approached the Philistine" (1 Sam. 17:38–40 NIV).

And you know the rest of the story. Rather than relying on his five smooth stones, David put his faith in "the name of the Lord Almighty" and defeated Goliath.

How often do we believe we need someone else's accessories or attributes to accomplish a task? If I had her platform, if I appeared more polished and put-together like her, if I only had her education or her resources.

But God, who is rich in mercy, has provided us with everything we need to fulfill the tasks He has assigned to us. There is no need to borrow someone else's battle (or fashion) gear; God has equipped us with our own armor, and it fits perfectly.

FORTY-EIGHT

Celebrate the Most Wonder-Full Time of Year

He learned to flip the switch that turned on the train. Together, we lay beside the Christmas tree, watching intently as the Polar Express made its way around the tree; round and round it chugged, whistling occasionally, with the conductor calling, "All aboard!" His little eyes were full of wonder, just like any two-year-old's.

She couldn't take her eyes off the twinkling lights of the Christmas tree. The wonder showed through her six-month-old little body, so still and focused, watching the colors change from bright white to red and then blue.

Observing the world through my grandchildren's eyes reignites that simple, childlike wonder. More marvelous than this gift, however, is contemplating the miracle of Jesus' birth. Each morning, when I read part of the Christmas story, I feel invited to pause and reflect. I read just a few verses at a time and take moments to wonder. I'm amazed by the precise timing of the events that needed to align for the prophecies to be fulfilled.

Micah foretold Jesus' birth 700 years before His arrival and specified the small town; this makes me stop and wonder.

Mary and Joseph didn't even live in Bethlehem; however, the first

115

census was instituted at just the right time. This required them to travel from their hometown of Nazareth and placed them in Bethlehem on the exact day of His birth. I am filled with wonder at the precision of the timing and all those involved in bringing this prophecy to fulfillment.

Astonishingly, many prophets in the Old Testament proclaimed Jesus' lineage, indicating that He would come from the line of Jesse, the father of King David. As I read through the record of Jesus' ancestors, I see that God divinely used murderers, prostitutes, the lowly, and those in power to bring about Jesus' earthly birth. Wow, God! This is truly amazing. It makes me stop and wonder.

This Advent, I embrace God's call to slow down and reflect. I read and ponder with great anticipation, waiting for God's quiet whispers. Like a child, I may not fully understand the mystery, yet I am filled with such awe that I watch and wait. The God who became flesh makes me stop and wonder.

FORTY-NINE

Celebrate Through Hurt and Conflict

After an emotionally draining weekend sorting through my parents' home and watching strangers cart off heirlooms and memories, I sat in the recliner at a friend's home, longing for a few moments of quiet and rest. I held a warm cup of tea for added comfort, and I picked up my phone to check for an update from an old friend coming for a visit. No news from her; however, I noticed an email had arrived from one of my dearest friends of many years.

She was a shelter through many storms, and her infectious laughter brought untold joy to my life. I loved the way we complemented each other. We were the poster children for the saying, "Opposites attract." She was smart and studious; I was funny and laid-back. She was a fashionista, while I was usually clad in sweats and a tee.

She had recently mentioned the idea of writing long emails to each other, a practice we had cherished long ago but hadn't engaged in recently. That sounded exciting! Then I began to read her long email. To say I was shocked and speechless would be an understatement.

After questioning my political views, on which we had not conversed about in eight years due to her passionate concern for current events and my nonchalant approach to something I truly have no control over—again, our "opposites attract" personalities—she then proceeded to question several of my core values and beliefs. After several more hurtful paragraphs, she concluded the email by writing, "I could just drift away, stop contacting you, let the friendship just slowly fade, but I thought I owed it to you to explain why."

The realization that my best friend was contemplating walking away from our decades-long, deeply committed friendship, primarily because of politics, was soul-crushing. I was in the middle of finishing the manuscript for this book and was already mentally and physically exhausted. Could I really find a reason to celebrate after reading her unsettling thoughts? I put down my phone, cuddled up with a blanket, and shed many tears. Finding the good in feeling hurt and betrayed would not come easily.

Given a few days, I began to reflect on our fond memories; they were a reason to celebrate. I contemplated the miles we trekked through foreign countries, the many varied cultural experiences, the prayer times as we lifted each other and those we love to the Father together, the milestone birthdays, and the numerous cups of tea we shared, the books we read and exchanged, our children's friendships, taxi rides through bustling cities, and quiet walks through the woods on our way to the rambunctious roar of magnificent waterfalls.

Yes, there are many reasons to celebrate. And there is still hope. Even though we have yet to reconcile, there is hope that Jesus will someday reunite our hearts and that our friendship will reflect His relentless "beauty from ashes" kind of grace. Hope brings a smile to the soul, and whenever it resides in our hearts, joy walks alongside us. In the midst of grief and sadness from loss, Jesus whispers, "There's always a reason to celebrate." We can trust the God who understands firsthand the pain of hurt and betrayal.

FIFTY

Celebrate When Your Daughter is Furloughed

Towards the end of my year of focusing on reasons to celebrate, my youngest daughter was unexpectedly furloughed from her first big-girl job after graduating from college during COVID. She was a real trooper, and though she was disappointed, she almost immediately began to search for a silver lining (and another job!).

Because she is 3,000 miles away, I decided to help keep her eyes fixed on Jesus and trust He has something better by sending her a package including a card that read, "Sometimes something good has to end so something better can come along."

I included a list titled "Top Twenty Things to Do When You're Furloughed," along with all the necessary items to accomplish these tasks. A few of her favorites were a Starbucks gift card, a box of tea, a candle, and a new book for a cozy evening at home; paper airplanes for her and her husband to assemble and see whose can fly the furthest; notecards, a new journal, and a few pretty pens; and a Food and Drink Trivia game so they could invite friends over for dinner and games.

Discouraged at times, she continued to fill out applications and search in all the right places. Thankfully, it wasn't long until she was offered a new job, but as she was searching, I needed to remind her that even in the tough times, there's always a reason to celebrate.

FIFTY-ONE

Celebrate the Secret to Knowing Jesus

I have a two-year-old in my life. She is just learning to talk and has unique ways of pronouncing words, making it sometimes difficult to decipher what she's saying. At first, I depended on her parents to translate for me.

Lately, however, I've discovered that the best way to understand her is to spend time with her. The longer I'm with her, the easier it becomes to figure out what she's saying. The more I listen to her, the better I get at learning her unique ways of communicating. Sometimes when I can't understand her words, I come to know what she means through her expressions and body language. The more I'm around her, the easier it is to understand what she wants me to know.

I met a new friend recently. She was so excited to tell me all about herself. We talked (she talked) for what seemed like thirty minutes before she took a breath. I just listened. As we parted ways, she apologized when she realized she had talked the whole time. While I left knowing a few things about her, she knew nothing about me.

I'm discovering there are two primary ways to get to know someone: by spending time with them and by listening. If your goal in a relationship is to know and understand the other person, it's essential to invest time together and listen more than you speak.

When I first started walking with Jesus, I relied on others to interpret what He was saying by listening to sermons and reading books, which is still a great way to hear from Him. However, now that I've spent time getting to know Him, it's even sweeter when I can hear what He's telling me without always depending on someone else to interpret.

I had lunch last week with a friend who, like me, has been around the block a few times and has come to understand and appreciate the value of spending time each day with Jesus. We concluded that it's not something you can really explain; it's something you must experience. Once you've experienced spending time with Jesus, you come to understand its value.

Another friend of mine has a saying: "You can't spend time with Jesus every day and not be changed." An author friend of mine expressed a similar idea when asked to define the word "abide": to abide is to sit at the feet of Jesus daily, listening to His words with a heart prepared to obey.

This is the key to a successful Christian life—spending time with Jesus every day.

In Philippians 3:10, Paul wrote, "I want to know Christ and experience the mighty power that raised Him from the dead." This desire will manifest uniquely in our lives as we navigate different seasons. I am currently in a season without children at home. I do not have a job that requires me to leave early in the morning, allowing me to prioritize spending time with Jesus first thing in the morning.

My normal routine involves going downstairs and ceremoniously making my tea (the way the Brits taught me), lighting my candles, and then sitting at His feet. I intentionally abide with Jesus every morning—sitting at His feet, reading His word, and listening to Him with a heart to obey.

I know many of you are in a season where you need to be at work early in the morning or have young children with you all the time, or both! I once heard someone say, "My children wake up at the crack of the Bible." I remember those days; at one point, I had five children under the age of eight, so I understand how hard it can be! While it may be more challenging for you to find ten minutes of alone time with Jesus, it's not impossible. It just takes intentionality.

During that busy season of my life, a mentor and friend introduced me to the idea of having a tent. She referred to Genesis 12:8, which reads, "From there he [Abram] moved to the hill country on the east of Bethel and pitched his tent, with Bethel on the west and Ai on the east. There he built an altar to the Lord and called upon the name of the Lord" (NIV). Bethel, which means "house of bread," symbolizes the church. Ai, which translates to "heap of ruins," can symbolize the world. Abram pitched his tent between the two, and there, he built an altar.

So, one way to spend time with Jesus is to get a tent. A tent can be any cute bag you choose to hold the contents of your "altar." My tent usually holds the following items: my Bible, a journal, a cute pen, a devotional or study I'm working on, a few notecards (in case the Lord prompts me to write a note to someone), a bottle of water, and always a few pieces of chocolate.

Make it a habit to carry your tent every time you leave the house. You may not know when you'll have ten minutes to pitch your tent as you go through your day. It might be while you're waiting at the dentist or doctor's office, in the carpool line waiting for a child, or in between other appointments. (Do yourself a huge favor: remove Facebook from your phone so you're not tempted to waste your time scrolling through it mindlessly. You've got more important things to do!)

The bottom line is this: spending time with Jesus every day will transform your life. Again, as my friend says, "You can't sit at the feet of Jesus every day and not be changed. It just happens!"

FIFTY-TWO
Celebrate Some Oatmeal with Pa

I t's time for breakfast, and my thoughts turn toward oatmeal. It was always a favorite growing up, although I was partial to my mom's version. It was never sticky or goopy, always smooth and a bit runny, with a sprinkle of brown sugar on top—like her signature kiss to bless a new day. Over the years, I added blueberries and nuts, and when I was home for a visit, my mom always made sure these new toppings were ready for my mornings spent with her and my dad.

Until six months before his passing, my dad played golf three days a week, rising early and leaving the house by 7:00 a.m. But the mornings he was home, I'd come downstairs and round the corner into the living room to see him dressed in a golf shirt and shorts (or in winter pants and a sweater, often with the fireplace flames warmly dancing), sitting in his recliner and playing the crossword puzzle in the Northwest Florida Daily News. We would exchange the same greeting, "Good morning, Pa!" to which he would reply, "How's it going, Girl?" I would then proceed to the kitchen to begin my tea-making routine. Within a few minutes, he would either ask me if I wanted an egg for breakfast (he made the best), or I would ask if he wanted oatmeal.

Most mornings, my mom would sit on the couch reading her Bible, observing our interactions but content not to interfere and let this be just dad-and-daughter time. Her heart delighted in watching my sisters and me spending time with my dad, none of us realizing the days were so fleeting and how important these small memories would be to carry us through our current days.

So today, as I'm making oatmeal, I'm thinking about my dad and missing him more than I do on most mornings. In my effort to relive those special moments, I call out as I gather the ingredients from the pantry, "Hey Pa, would you like some oatmeal this morning?" I yearn to hear him reply, "If you're making some, I'll have a bowl." I set out two bowls, measure the oatmeal, and turn on the stove. Then I reach for my mom's wooden spoon, perfectly aged from stirring numerous bowls of oatmeal and the source of my fondest memories—one of the many treasures I brought home after her passing. Lastly, I sprinkle a teaspoon of brown sugar on top: a kiss from my mom that blesses this day.

Appendix

The following thoughts are from my daughter, a missionary in Africa who could not make it home to say goodbye to her grandparents.

I am by no means an expert on grief, having suffered very little in this life. It seems to me that grief is very much a kind of school, and as those to whom it has been promised that we will suffer, should we indeed live godly lives, any such painful trial proves to be a golden opportunity to lean on and learn from Jesus, the humble Savior who suffered greatly for us yet without sin. So Jesus, teach each of us through this most recent grief; draw us nearer to You, the Suffering Servant. In looking to Jesus through this pain, I feel as though He has invited me into a two-fold tasting of His heart: one, in remembrance, and two, in surrendering my current and future days.

That first invitation from our Lord is a cherished remembrance of my Grammy and Grandaddy's lives. I truly believe it honors my Heavenly Father when I take little moments to thank Him for the sweet memories I shared with them. This recognition can arise at any time: When I catch a glimpse of the hands of an elderly woman, my mind always returns to Grammy's disfigured, yet soft and gentle fingers, and I thank God for the ways He used those hands to bless many. I think of her at eighty-nine years of age, writing in her beautiful cursive on birthday cards and prayer requests displayed on her fridge chalkboard, even with failing sight and trembling hands.

When my children hear the ticking of the clock, we recall the joyful surprise of the German figures popping out of Grammy and Grandaddy's many clocks to announce the hour. Any time I see Mountain Dew, it reminds me of how willing Grandaddy was, even in his weak health, to rise from his rocker and head to the garage to offer us a cold drink in the heat of Florida summers. I remember Grandaddy's generosity when he gave me his guitar the moment he heard I wanted to learn to play. I think of the smell of humid air after storms and recall the hours spent waiting at Grammy and Grandaddy's for the thunderstorm to pass so we could enjoy childhood thrills at Lincoln Park. To dwell on these reflections and offer sacrifices of thanksgiving is something I believe pleases the Lord.

The second is like it—as I reflect on how quickly, even with the anticipation that comes from the blessing of old age, death arrived so suddenly, I must humbly admit my life is not my own. My days are numbered by my Good Father, and He invites me to live totally surrendered to Him until He calls me home. May Grammy and Grandaddy's lives and the grief over their deaths be a cause for joyful thanksgiving and sober surrender to the One who laid down His life in death and overcame in resurrection, offering us forgiveness of sins for those who repent, and eternal hope in life and death.

Mallory (Husfelt) Nieveen
Chad, Africa
August 2024

About the Author

Award-winning author and blogger, Michele Husfelt has traveled the world first as an Air Force kid and then as an Air Force spouse, living in 36 different homes in five countries. She loved her military childhood so much that she never wanted to leave. Gratefully, she fell in love with a fellow Florida State Seminole who felt a call into the military chaplaincy, and together they served 34 years before Chaplain Mike traded in his BDUs for rural church pastor attire. Today, he pastors Upperville Baptist Church in the wine and horse countryside an hour west of D.C.

Michele and Mike have five funny kids, four fortunate sons-in-law, and six bubbly grands (aged seven and under) who live in various locations between Seattle and Africa. They also share their home with a perfect Goldendoodle, Hazel Grace.

In addition to writing and editing for various publications, Michele has spoken at numerous events across the globe, sharing her passion for godly friendships, creating community, and loving her neighbors. In her spare time, she loves to sit on her front porch with a cup of tea and a good (or new) friend. You can find Michele at whitesandandteacups.com (two of her favorite things).

Acknowledgments

Writing can be a lonely task. The secret to making it bearable is to find others who have the same calling and spend time writing together in community. Along the way, I have been blessed to find a few fellow writers and others who have been encouragers and motivators:

Thank you to Katie Harding, who has been a fellow writer, cherished friend, and co-laborer in our small slice of kingdom work. She has simultaneously praised my work and challenged my thoughts, pushing me (some days uphill both ways) to pen my words with authenticity and vulnerability. It hasn't always been an easy road. Thank you, Katie, for believing it was worth it.

Thank you to my mentor and friend, Cynthia Heald, who has invested in me for more than two decades. Through her writing and the many cups of tea we sipped on her patio and in other places, Cynthia has taught me from her studies, but more importantly, from sharing her everyday life, the qualities that make a woman of excellence.

Thank you to Michele Bowden and Hulda Bennett for great coffee shop dates and for making the writing space less lonely.

Thank you to Ronda Sturgill, one of my Brighton Sisters, for all the edits and the inspiration to continue down dirt roads, even when your wheelchair tires get bogged down in the mud. You are a real treasure.

Thank you to the rest of my Brighton Sisters: Rhonda Robinson, Kari Alley, and Terri Carter. We've traveled many years together, and each year gets better and better.

Thank you to my BFFs I picked up along our various military duty stations: Colleen Paige, Jan Schiller, Sharon (Nicole) Egan, Kathy Dooley, Sherry Howard, Lindsey Kindt, and Monica (from church) Burchell.

Thank you to my daughters in the Lord: Madison Jimas, Phoebe Drybola, Kendra Smith, Heather Harvey, Sara Field, Sydney Hampton, Savanna Schaefer, Debra Peake, Kailyn Van Schooten, and Alexa Panaccione. Thank you for letting me be a part of your young lives.

Thank you to those who cheered me on as I wrote. These are the people I always thought, "If I ever write a book, I want to thank these friends publicly": Denise Schaick, Michelle Foust, Paula Dixon, Maureen Kovach, Phyllis Wilson, Karen Madruga, Doris Lama, and Sandy Troutman.

Thank you to my NorthStar family and fellow staff members: Bryan Jones, Mike Bradley, Katie Harding, Mary Beth Inman, Dawn Groves, Jennifer Stovall, and Eloise Barton. I have been stretched and grown and have loved working with you all to "energize churches as they carry out their God-given vision." Only God knew how much I needed each of you.

Thank you to my final proofreader and Upperville neighbor, Kathleen Ambrose. I'm honored that you generously shared your time and talent, and most importantly, I'm grateful for your friendship.

Finally, thank you to Kim Blackaby, my soulmate for so many years. Little did we know the adventures that lay ahead as we forged our friendship so long ago. As a fellow writer, ministry leader, minister's wife, and follower of Jesus, I am forever grateful for the gift of you in my life. May Jesus continue to grow us as He writes the rest of our story.

The cover photo was captured at one of Michele's fondest childhood memory-making spots, Lincoln Park, on Tom's Bayou in Valparaiso, Florida. On that particular day many years ago, the jumpers happened to be her four daughters, visiting their grandparents and reliving Michele's joy of small-town life on the bayou.

The original seven in 2015. L-R Emilie, Lydia, Michele, Bro. Mike, Elijah, Mallory, Britain (photo credit: Kathy Dooley)

Bro Mike's AF retirement ceremony in 2023. L-R Michael, Emilie, Rhett; (in back - Malone & Britain); Drew, Courtland, Mallory, Elizabeth; Michele with Charlotte and Mike; Eli and Bea; Lydia, Hannah, Jonah, Zac (photo credit: Mike Harding)